CAMPAIGN 417

SECOND SIRTE 1942

The Desperate Battle to Relieve Malta

ANGUS KONSTAM ILLUSTRATED BY ADAM TOOBY

OSPREY PUBLISHING
Bloomsbury Publishing Plc
Kemp House, Chawley Park, Cumnor Hill, Oxford OX2 9PH, UK
Bloomsbury Publishing Ireland Limited,
29 Earlsfort Terrace, Dublin 2, D02 AY28, Ireland
1385 Broadway, 5th Floor, New York, NY 10018, USA
E-mail: info@ospreypublishing.com
www.ospreypublishing.com

OSPREY is a trademark of Osprey Publishing Ltd

First published in Great Britain in 2025

© Osprey Publishing Ltd, 2025

All rights reserved. No part of this publication may be: i) reproduced or transmitted in any form, electronic or mechanical, including photocopying, recording or by means of any information storage or retrieval system without prior permission in writing from the publishers; or ii) used or reproduced in any way for the training, development or operation of artificial intelligence (AI) technologies, including generative AI technologies. The rights holders expressly reserve this publication from the text and data mining exception as per Article 4(3) of the Digital Single Market Directive (EU) 2019/790

A catalogue record for this book is available from the British Library.

ISBN: PB 9781472867223; eBook 9781472867193; ePDF 9781472867209; XML 9781472867216

25 26 27 28 29   10 9 8 7 6 5 4 3 2 1

Maps by Bounford.com
3D BEVs by Paul Kime
Index by Angela Hall
Typeset by PDQ Digital Media Solutions, Bungay, UK
Printed by Repro India Ltd

Osprey Publishing supports the Woodland Trust, the UK's leading woodland conservation charity.

To find out more about our authors and books visit www.ospreypublishing.com. Here you will find extracts, author interviews, details of forthcoming events and the option to sign up for our newsletter.

For product safety related questions contact productsafety@bloomsbury.com

Front cover main illustration: R. Adm. Vian's flagship HMS *Cleopatra* is hit, 22 March 1942. (Adam Tooby)
Title page image: The Dido-class cruisers HMS *Euryalus* and HMS *Cleopatra* on 11 March 1942, fending off an Axis air attack during a passage from Malta to Alexandria. (Stratford Archive)

Photographs
Unless otherwise stated, the images in this book are from the Stratford Archive.

Author's note
Distances in this book are usually given in nautical miles (nm), where 1 mile equates to 2,025yds (1,852m). In gunnery, though, during this period a mile was measured as 2,000yds (1,829m).

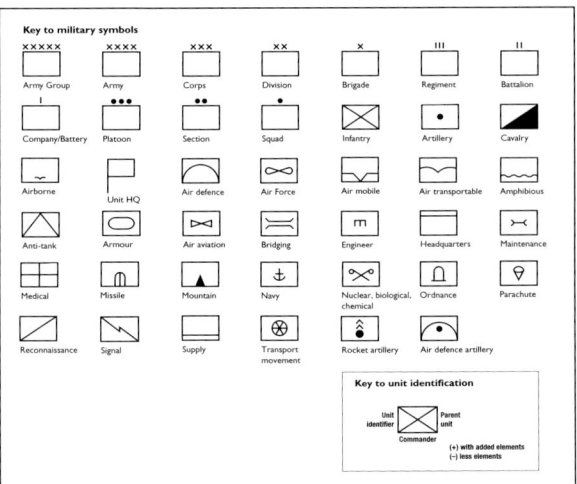

CONTENTS

INTRODUCTION	4
CHRONOLOGY	7
ORIGINS OF THE CAMPAIGN	9
OPPOSING COMMANDERS	15
The Royal Navy ▪ The Regia Marina	
OPPOSING FORCES	20
The Royal Navy ▪ The Regia Marina ▪ Orders of battle	
OPPOSING PLANS	26
The Royal Navy ▪ The Regia Marina	
THE CAMPAIGN	32
Operation *MG-1* ▪ D-Day and D+1 ▪ 'Enemy driven off' ▪ Second contact 'The Medina Melee' ▪ The final leg	
AFTERMATH	89
THE BATTLEFIELD TODAY	93
FURTHER READING	94
INDEX	95

INTRODUCTION

On the face of it, Second Sirte was a strange name for an important battle. Before World War II, Sirte itself was described as 'a shabby little Arab village of mud huts', which was sited on the coast some 200 miles east of Tripoli. After the war, it became a city following the discovery of oil in the desert. However, in 1942 it was a nondescript dot on the map. That dot, though, gave its name to the Gulf of Sirte, a huge bowl-shaped dip in the North African coast, 550 miles across and 150 miles high. During the war, this became hugely important as it lay at the African end of the vital sea route between mainland Italy and its Libyan colony. The British knew this and did whatever they could to disrupt the flow of tanks, men and supplies intended to reinforce their German and Italian foes in the Western Desert. The British, however, had their own vulnerable Achilles' heel.

The key to Britain's campaign was Malta. The fortress island once described as the 'The Verdun of the Mediterranean' stood like a bastion astride these vital Axis supply routes. The Axis recognized its importance and subjected the island to one of the most sustained aerial bombing offensives of the war. Malta's survival centred on supplies: the food, fuel and ammunition the islanders and its garrison needed to survive – and to fight on. This meant that both the British and the Italians had vital supplies to transport through the contested waters of the central Mediterranean.

Rubble blocking the street in Valletta. Malta was subjected to one of the most prolonged and intensive aerial bombardments of the war, by both Italian and German bombers. By the spring of 1942, the survival of the fortress island was in doubt, unless supplies of food, fuel and munitions could be shipped to it.

The Italian battleships *Conte di Cavour* and *Giulio Cesare* lying at anchor in Malta's Valletta harbour, during a goodwill visit there in 1938. At this stage, the growing power of Italy's Regia Marina didn't greatly concern the British, as its own Mediterranean Fleet based in Malta had the support of the French Marine Nationale. France's defeat in the spring of 1940 left the British to face the Italian threat on its own.

The British sea routes to Malta converged on the island from both the east and the west, while the Italians' own convoys passed through the same waters from north to south. For both sides, victory in the Mediterranean meant the safeguarding of their own supply routes, while blocking those of the enemy.

The British faced the harder task. The presence of powerful German and Italian air formations in Sicily, Libya, Greece and Crete meant that British convoys had to run the gauntlet of near-incessant air attacks. In the spring of 1942, the British Mediterranean Fleet based in Alexandria had been weakened by losses to Axis aircraft and submarines, and was heavily outnumbered by the Italian fleet. As a result, it had effectively lost control of the central Mediterranean. This made the running of small, fast supply convoys through to Malta an extremely dangerous business. In December 1941, one such convoy from Alexandria to Malta provoked a clash with the Italian battlefleet at the First Battle of Sirte. Although this battle was indecisive, the British fast supply ship at the heart of the convoy made it through to Malta. However, the battle demonstrated a new-found resolve by the Italian fleet, if amply supported by aircraft.

In late March 1942, the British tried again. R. Adm. Sir Philip Vian led the operation, relying on light forces to outmanoeuvre the Italians and run supplies through to Malta from the east. Forewarned, the Italian battlefleet put to sea to stop the British. Just as it did the previous December, the two sides met some 200 miles south-east of Malta, just off the north-eastern approaches to the Gulf of Sirte. As before then, the 'village of mud huts' gave its name to a naval battle, fought some 200 miles to its north. For the British, there was a lot at stake. The very survival of Malta rode on the outcome, and with it the Allied ability to maintain a foothold in the central Mediterranean. What followed was a David and Goliath struggle, where Vian used bluff and manoeuvre to counter the Italians' superiority in strength and numbers. The result was one of the most dramatic naval encounters of World War II.

For years afterwards, historians and naval analysts have argued about who won the Second Battle of Sirte. Vian's defence of the convoy against almost overwhelming odds was masterly. Over the course of the day, he successfully kept the Italians from attacking the convoy, and by nightfall the Italian battlefleet broke off the action. This delayed the convoy, so that at dawn the following day it was still at sea, making its final approach to Malta. There, the four merchant ships that made up the convoy were all

By late March 1942, after one of the heaviest bomber offensives of the war, much of Valletta, Malta's capital, lay in ruins, and its inhabitants reduced to living in cellars or shelters. This is the remains of Valletta's Royal Opera House, destroyed in early 1942.

picked off by Axis aircraft. So, while the battle was a textbook feat of convoy defence by Vian's force, the whole operation was a strategic failure. The Axis stranglehold around Malta remained as tight as ever, and the harrowing siege continued. This, then, is the story of this dramatic naval clash, where both sides emerged with laurels, but the outcome did little for the starving people of Malta.

CHRONOLOGY

1941

18 November	Operation *Crusader* begins – British drive to relieve Tobruk.
19 November	Force K (Malta Strike Force) runs into minefield – light cruiser *Neptune* sunk, *Aurora* and *Penelope* damaged and destroyer *Kandahar* forced to scuttle.
25 November	Battleship HMS *Barham* sunk off Egyptian coast by U-boat.
10 December	Tobruk relieved – Germans withdraw from Cyrenaica.
14 December	Cruiser HMS *Galatea* sunk off Alexandria by German U-boat.
17 December	First Battle of Sirte – R. Adm. Vian protects British fast one-ship convoy, but Adm. Iachino successfully protects his own Libya-bound convoy.
18 December	Auxiliary supply ship HMS *Breconshire* reaches Malta.
19 December	Battleships HMS *Queen Elizabeth* and HMS *Valiant* disabled by daring Italian 'human torpedo' attack in Alexandria harbour.
25 December	British troops enter Benghazi.
	Fliegerkorps II transferred from Russia to Sicily.

1942

21 January	Rommel launches counter-offensive at El Agheila.
2 February	British establish defensive line at Gazala, west of Tobruk.
14 February	British convoy from Alexandria fails to make it through to Malta due to Axis air attack.
11 March	Cruiser HMS *Naiad* sunk off Crete by U-boat.
15 March	British cruisers bombard Rhodes.
18 March	5th Destroyer Flotilla sails from Alexandria for ASW sweep.
20 March (D-Day)	Escort destroyer HMS *Heythrop* sunk off Bardia by U-boat.
	Convoy MW-10 sails from Alexandria, followed in the evening by Force B.
20–22 March	RAF and FAA bombing raids of Axis airfields in Cyrenaica.
21 March (D+1)	5th Destroyer Flotilla and then Force B rendezvous with convoy.
	(Force B temporarily redesignated as Covering Force.)
	Convoy spotted by German aircraft and Italian submarine.
	Force K puts to sea from Alexandria.
22 March (D+2)	
0100hrs	Italian battlefleet spotted off Taranto by British submarine *P-36*.
0800hrs	Force K join's R. Adm. Vian's Covering Force.
0900hrs	Air cover ends for convoy as RAF fighters reach limit of their range.

Second Battle of Sirte (Sunday 22 March 1941)

0930hrs	First air attack on convoy. These attacks would continue throughout the day.
1330hrs	Italian floatplane sighted by British, suggesting Italian battlefleet was nearby.

1417hrs	Italian ships first sighted to north by HMS *Euryalus*.
1420hrs	Vian puts Covering Force on defensive posture.
1435hrs	Italian cruisers open fire on British cruisers.
1456hrs	Vian orders British cruisers to return fire.
1515hrs	Both sides cease fire, ending first clash of the battle.
1618hrs	Adm. Iachino rendezvouses with V. Adm. Parona's cruiser force.
1640hrs	Italian battlefleet sighted by HMS *Euryalus*.
1643hrs	Iachino opens fire on British cruisers.
1645hrs	Vian's flagship HMS *Cleopatra* hit.
1648hrs	British cruisers withdraw into smokescreen and break contact.
1706hrs	Italians temporarily cease fire due to lack of clear targets.
1720hrs	Smoke thins and Italians resume firing. Destroyer HMS *Havock* hit.
1744hrs	Clash between 22nd Destroyer Flotilla and *Littorio*.
1750hrs	British cruisers reappear and exchange fire with *Littorio*.
1806hrs	HMS *Cleopatra* fires torpedoes and is then hit abaft the bridge.
1820hrs	Iachino resumes attempt to intercept convoy.
1834hrs	14th Destroyer Flotilla sights *Littorio* and commences torpedo attack.
1841hrs	Destroyer HMS *Kingston* hit and temporarily disabled.
1842hrs	14th Destroyer Flotilla launches its torpedoes and Italian battlefleet turns away.
1851hrs	22nd Destroyer Flotilla launches torpedoes at *Littorio* as it withdraws.
1855hrs	Iachino orders his battlefleet to cease fire, ending the battle.
1900hrs	Convoy disperses before the final leg of the voyage to Malta. Cruiser HMS *Carlisle* and 5th Destroyer Flotilla divided to support the merchantmen.
2000hrs	Covering Force withdraws (becoming Force B again). Force K together with damaged destroyers HMS *Havock* and HMS *Kingston* are detached from Force B, and ordered to reach Malta.

Monday 23 March

0720hrs	First air attacks of morning, targeting merchant ship SS *Clan Campbell*.
0835hrs	Air attacks on M/S *Talabot* and MV *Pampas* as they approach Valletta.
0900–1000hrs	*Talabot* and *Pampas* anchor in Valletta's Grand Harbour.
0920hrs	HMS *Breconshire* damaged in air attack. It is eventually brought to anchor in a bay on south-east side of Malta.
1020hrs	*Clan Campbell* attacked and sunk by German bombers, 50 miles from Malta. Survivors rescued by escort destroyer HMS *Eridge*.
1130hrs	Destroyer *Legion* damaged in air attack, but successfully brought to anchor near *Breconshire*.

ORIGINS OF THE CAMPAIGN

On the evening of 9 May 1940, Nazi Germany launched *Fall Gelb* (*Case Yellow*), the invasion of France and the Low Countries. At that moment, though few realized it, the expansion of the war into the Mediterranean became all but inevitable. By enticing the British and much of the French army into Belgium, the Germans were able to pin the Allies to the east of Brussels, while the bulk of their mobile troops advanced through the Ardennes region, which Allied planners had deemed virtually impassable to a modern army. Then, after establishing a bridgehead over the River Meuse near Sedan, the German panzers spearheaded a 'blitzkrieg' advance across northern France. By 20 May, the Germans had reached the English Channel, and had divided the Allied armies in two. The Allies in Belgium were forced to withdraw to the coast, and within a week the evacuation of Dunkirk had begun. By 4 June, the Germans had turned south, and were driving on Paris.

It was now clear that Paris would fall, and France would be defeated. On 10 June, the opportunistic Italian dictator Benito Mussolini declared war on Britain and France. This seemingly impulsive move dramatically widened the scope of the war. Britain controlled Egypt, Malta and Gibraltar, and maintained a sizeable Mediterranean Fleet, which was immediately placed on a war footing. After all, the fleet's main base at Malta was now less than 70 miles from Italian airfields in Sicily, and 300 miles from the Italian fleet's main base at Taranto. On 22 June, the French signed an armistice with Germany, and two days later another was signed with Italy. With France knocked out of the war, Britain had lost its major ally in the Mediterranean theatre. Worse, it now faced the spectre of France's North African possessions as well as the chance of its fleet coming under German control.

In the 1930s, when Italy dramatically expanded the size of its fleet, naval balance was maintained by the combined British and French fleets keeping a parity with the Italians. Now, with France defeated, the Royal Navy's Mediterranean Fleet found itself badly outnumbered. Consequently, it abandoned its base in Malta and the fleet moved to Alexandria in Egypt, some 830 miles to the east. A smaller naval

Adm. Iachino, welcoming Benito Mussolini and a group of Italian officers on board the flagship *Littorio* in Taranto. While Iachino, a skilled commander, was eager to use his battlefleet to protect Axis convoys and to intercept British ones, Mussolini and the Supermarina (the Italian naval high command) – were risk-averse, and cited lack of fuel as a reason for limiting the battlefleet's sorties in the wake of Matapan.

group dubbed Force H was stationed in Gibraltar. Malta remained under British control, and the coming of war placed it at the forefront of the naval campaign. British supply routes ran east to west across the Mediterranean, while Italy's supply routes to Libya ran from north to south. Malta stood virtually at the spot where these two routes crossed. Inevitably, the island fortress would assume an important role in the fighting.

From June to December 1940, the two fleets clashed inconclusively, off Punta Stilo in Calabria and Spartivento in Sicily, but it was the Fleet Air Arm attack on Taranto in late November that tipped the balance in Britain's favour. The Italian battlefleet was attacked by Swordfish biplanes launched from HMS *Illustrious*, sinking two battleships and forcing a third to run aground to prevent its loss. At a stroke, half of Italy's battlefleet had been put out of action. However, it was off Matapan in March 1941 that Britain's Mediterranean Fleet was able to strike a telling blow. Adm. Cunningham's fleet overpowered its Italian adversaries led by Adm. Iachino in a dramatic night action, which ended in the loss of three Italian cruisers and two destroyers, as well as torpedo damage to an Italian battleship. After Matapan, it appeared that the Italian Navy had lost its nerve.

This, though, was an illusion – the result of caution imposed on the Supermarina by Mussolini. As Iachino demanded, it also represented a need for the navy to learn from its lessons, especially in the areas of naval and air force cooperation and adequate reconnaissance. Then, just a few weeks later, the whole strategic situation was turned on its head. In April 1941, the Germans invaded Yugoslavia and then Greece. The British sent troops to mainland Greece, but by the end of the month these had to be evacuated, in an embarrassing repeat of Dunkirk. But worse was to come. On 20 May, the Germans invaded Crete and were able to reinforce their troops thanks to their complete superiority in the air. The German Luftwaffe's Fliegerkorps VIII didn't just support the fighting on the ground – it also pounded the Royal Navy as the Mediterranean Fleet did what it could to support the Allied garrison on Crete.

Eventually, on 28 May, Cunningham's warships were called in to evacuate the defeated Allied troops, despite mounting casualties in ships and men. Although the bulk of these troops reached Egypt, Crete was lost, and the *Fliegerkorps* could then dominate the waters of the eastern Mediterranean. The Crete campaign had cost the Royal Navy dearly – four cruisers and six destroyers had been sunk or wrecked, and a carrier, two battleships and several more cruisers and destroyers were damaged. It would take several months to rebuild the Mediterranean Fleet, and in the meantime the Luftwaffe controlled the skies over the eastern Mediterranean.

Meanwhile, the defeat of the Italians in North Africa in the winter of 1940/41 almost ended the Desert War before it had properly begun. The arrival of Erwin Rommel and his Deutsches Afrika Korps in February 1941 gave the Italians a breathing space. Then, in March 1941, Rommel struck, and taken off balance the British and their Commonwealth allies were driven back 400 miles to the Egyptian border. A Commonwealth garrison remained at Tobruk, which was besieged until November. Then, after several failed attempts, the British 8th Army drove Rommel back to his starting point of the previous spring, near El Agheila (Al Aquayla) on the Gulf of Sirte. In January 1942, Rommel launched his second offensive, but this time the British and their allies held him around Gazala, to the west of Tobruk. There, both sides paused to take breath, and to resupply their troops.

The view from the open bridge of the Dido-class AA cruiser HMS *Euryalus* during the battle on 22 March 1942. In front of the cruiser is a sister ship, HMS *Cleopatra*, flagship of R. Adm. Vian, which is busily laying a smoke screen.

After the fall of Crete, the focus of the action shifted to the central Mediterranean. Both sides were heavily reliant on supply by sea, with the Italians operating convoys between Italian and Libyan ports. The main route between Naples and Tripoli was augmented by a secondary one to the east, from Taranto to Benghazi. For the British, if Malta was to remain in Allied hands then it needed to be resupplied, either from Alexandria to the east or Gibraltar to the west. In both cases, these British convoys would have to run the gauntlet of Axis air attacks from squadrons based in Sardinia, Sicily and Crete. The waters around Malta were also heavily mined by the Axis, and Italian and German submarines patrolled the approaches to the fortress island. Then there was the threat of an attack by the Italian battlefleet, based in Taranto.

For their part, the British relied on a submarine flotilla based in Valletta to attack the Axis convoy routes to Libya, supported by Force K, a small but highly effective naval strike force, which was also based in Malta. From October 1941, Force K punched well above its weight. In early November, Italian convoys to Tripoli were suspended after Force K destroyed the well-protected 'Beta' (or *Duisburg*) convoy. That month, over 60 per cent of Axis supplies shipped from Italy to Libya were lost to either Force K or British submarines. Damage to the British warships and the increased effectiveness of the air bombardment of Malta, however, led to the withdrawal of these surface ships. By the following March, all that remained of Force K was the light cruiser *Penelope* and the destroyer *Legion*.

More setbacks followed for the British. In November, the battleship *Barham* was sunk off the Egyptian coast by a German U-boat. Then, in December, a daring attack on Alexandria harbour by Italian midget submarines put the battleships *Queen Elizabeth* and *Valiant* out of action for several months, leaving Adm. Cunningham hard pressed to offer a counter to any Italian naval offensive. All that he could do was to concentrate on supplying Malta, using whatever light forces remained at his disposal.

The modern Italian battleship *Littorio*, flagship of Adm. Iachino, formed the core of his small but powerful battlefleet at Second Sirte. Armed with nine 15in guns in three triple turrets, *Littorio* was more than capable of destroying any warship encountered.

In mid-December, R. Adm. Vian left Alexandria to escort HMS *Breconshire* through to Malta. *Breconshire* was a former cargo liner converted into a fast tanker specifically for the Malta run. For this operation, it had been disguised as a battleship.

Late on 17 December, in rough seas and poor visibility, Vian encountered a powerful Italian surface force, some 200 miles north of Benghazi. It was Adm. Iachino's battlefleet, which was there to cover Axis convoy M-42's passage from Taranto to Tripoli and Benghazi. Vian's four cruisers and 12 destroyers were hopelessly outgunned by Iachino's three battleships, two cruisers and ten destroyers. Still, in the brief exchange that followed, Vian sidestepped the Italians and broke contact. Iachino, fearing a night attack on his own convoy, withdrew to protect it, leaving *Breconshire* and Vian's force to press on into Malta. This encounter was given the imposing name of the First Battle of Sirte, but in reality it was little more than a skirmish. Still, it reflected a greater willingness by the Italian fleet to offer battle, at least if the circumstances and numerical odds were in its favour.

Afterwards, both sides claimed victory. Post-war Italian naval historian Marco Bragadin claimed that, 'The *Littorio* group had taken the offensive for a whole day against a British group and had forced it to retire.' This of course was fatuous – the fight lasted 11 minutes, and consisted of nothing more than long-range fire from Iachino's flagship *Littorio* and two cruisers. Both sides managed to protect their convoys and push them through to their destinations. If anything the clash displayed a reluctance by the Italians to risk fighting in the dark. The British advantage of radar as well as their expertise in night fighting gave them a considerable advantage, and after Matapan the Italians knew it.

For the British, the first weeks of 1942 brought further problems. In early January, General Auchinleck's 8th Army's advance through Cyrenaica ground to a halt due to a lack of supplies. In contrast, two large Axis convoys had reached Libya, bringing fresh supplies and reinforcements for Rommel. His counter-attack, launched on 21 January, saw the 8th Army driven back to Gazala. This in turn enabled the Luftwaffe to station aircraft in Cyrenaica as well as in Crete and Greece, which then allowed Fliegerkorps II to dominate the eastern sea approaches to Malta. Soon these waters were

HMS *Cleopatra* was the flagship of R. Adm. Vian, commander of Force B, which became the Covering Force for Convoy MW-10 during the operation. Although designed primarily as AA ships, the ten 5.25in guns mounted in these Dido-class cruisers proved surprisingly effective against surface targets.

referred to as 'Bomb Alley' by the men of the Royal Navy. Meanwhile, Malta itself was subjected to increasing air attack, and the supply situation there was growing critical.

Still, Cunningham was determined that the running of fast supply ships through to Malta from the east would continue, while similar convoy attempts would be made from Gibraltar. In early January, the fast fleet auxiliary tanker HMS *Glengyle* reached Malta, escorted by Vian, and *Breconshire* was brought safely back to Alexandria. A few weeks later, Vian successfully escorted a small fast convoy of four ships through to Malta, although one of the merchantmen was sunk in an air attack as it approached the island. On 14 February, as Vian was escorting another three-ship fast convoy to Malta, reconnaissance planes of Fliegerkorps II spotted it to the east of Malta. It was then subjected to a series of heavy air attacks, which resulted in two of the freighters sunk, and the third, SS *Clan Campbell*, damaged and forced to put in to Tobruk.

It was clear that the Luftwaffe was making good use of their recaptured airfields in North Africa. However, in late February another operation saw the successful extraction of *Glengyle* and the running of *Breconshire* safely into Malta. Part of this success was down to air support, provided to Vian by the Royal Air Force (RAF). This helped limit the threat posed by the German bombers. It was evident that any future fast convoy run needed to be well planned and given all the support Cunningham and Vian could muster.

First, though, in early March Cunningham ordered Vian to go onto the offensive. Two Italian convoys were at sea, heading to and from Tripoli. On 10 March, Vian left Alexandria to intercept them, and to collect the AA cruiser *Cleopatra*, which had just reached Malta from Britain. However, on the 11th, Vian's flagship *Naiad* was torpedoed off the Crete coast by a German U-boat, and the rest of the force was subjected to heavy air attacks. Although the enemy convoys were not intercepted, Vian managed to shepherd *Cleopatra* and the destroyer *Kingston* from Malta and bring them safely into Alexandria. *Cleopatra* duly replaced *Naiad* as Vian's flagship. This, though, did little to help the beleaguered island of Malta, the survival of which rested on the running of supplies through to it. This became the next priority for Cunningham and Vian – to plan another fast convoy, and fight it through to Malta in the face of everything the Luftwaffe and the Regia Marina could do to prevent its safe arrival.

The strategic situation in the central Mediterranean, spring 1942

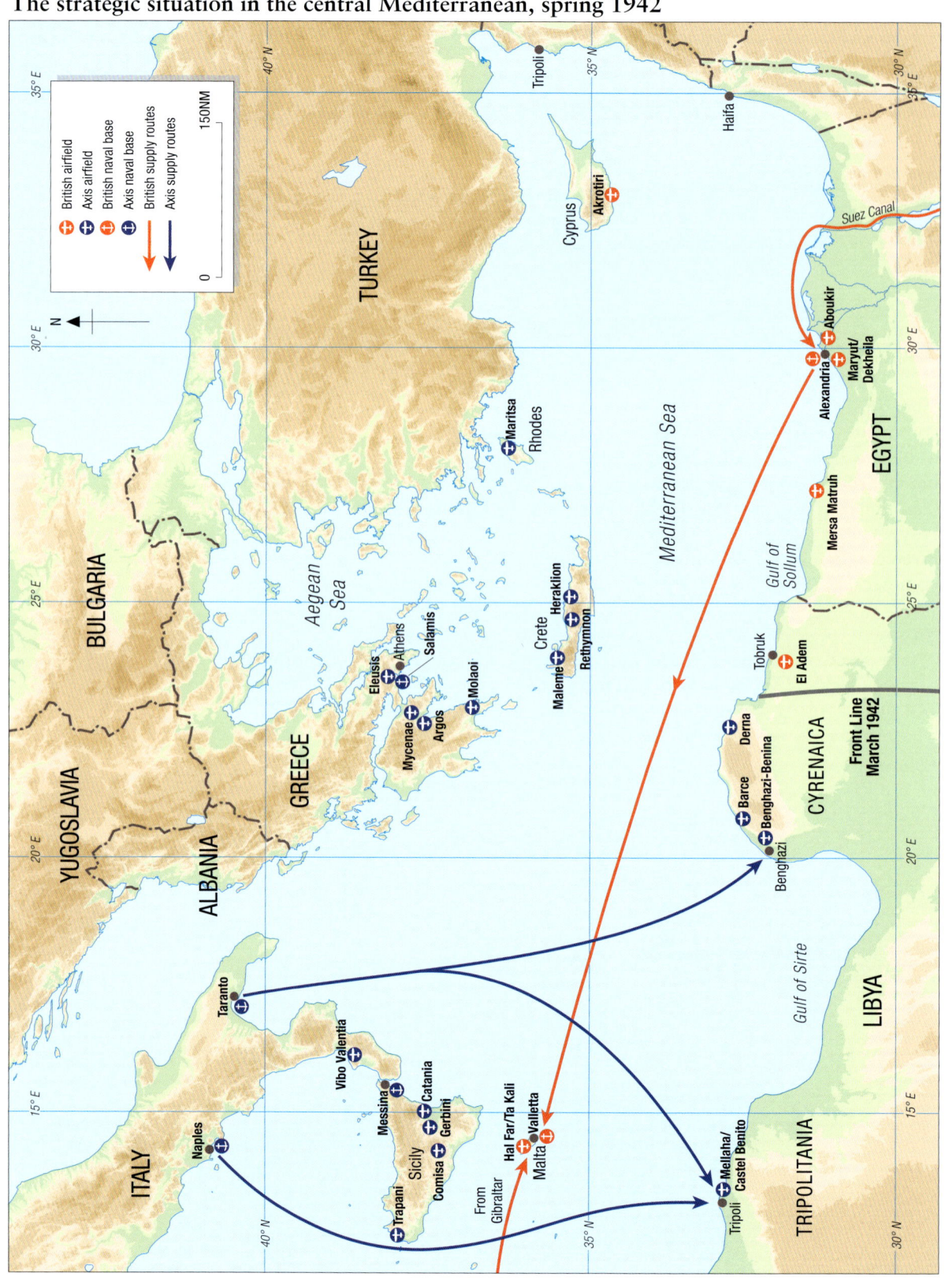

OPPOSING COMMANDERS

THE ROYAL NAVY

Since June 1939, the Royal Navy's Mediterranean Fleet had been under the command of **Admiral Sir Andrew B. Cunningham** (1883–1963), or 'ABC' as he was known. It helped that he was an 'old hand' in the Mediterranean, having served as the fleet's second-in-command during the late 1930s. Cunningham was born in Dublin, schooled in Edinburgh and joined the Navy as a naval cadet when he was 14. In 1908, as a lieutenant, he was given command of a torpedo boat. At the start of World War I, Cunningham commanded the destroyer HMS *Scorpion* in the Mediterranean, where he saw action at Gallipoli. He ended the war as a commander, with a reputation for sound judgement and decisiveness.

He went on to serve in the Baltic under Adm. Cowan and was given command of a destroyer flotilla. During the inter-war years, he married, and held various appointments afloat and ashore. In 1932, Cunningham was promoted to flag rank, becoming Rear Admiral (Destroyers) in the Mediterranean Fleet. He remained in the Mediterranean until 1938, when,

Adm. Andrew B. Cunningham, Commander-in-Chief of Britain's Mediterranean Fleet, pictured on board his flagship HMS *Warspite*. An extremely able and highly respected commander, 'ABC' was determined that despite lacking operational capital ships, he would do whatever it took to send supplies through the eastern Mediterranean to Malta.

R. Adm. Philip Vian wasn't a commander to suffer fools gladly and expected utter professionalism from his subordinates. However, he managed to build his captains into a Nelsonian 'band of brothers', who knew exactly what was expected of them when they went into action.

as a vice admiral, he was appointed to serve in the Admiralty. However, the following year, with war clouds looming, Cunningham was named Commander-in-Chief of the Mediterranean Fleet. Cunningham thoroughly understood the strategic and political demands of this theatre and had his fleet train for what he considered the likely event that Italy would be its main opponent.

When Italy entered the war, Cunningham moved his fleet to Alexandria and set about establishing his own fleet's dominance over the Regia Marina. The attack on Taranto in November 1940 was part of this, and his victory over the Italian fleet at Matapan the following March largely achieved this strategic goal. However, the subsequent intervention of the Luftwaffe and the fall of Greece and Crete completely undermined Cunningham's achievements. For the rest of 1941 and much of 1942, Cunningham's fleet was placed on the defensive. His resolution in the face of losses during the Crete operation marked Cunningham as a commander who understood the importance of his strategic role.

As a fleet admiral Cunningham drove himself and his subordinates hard and expected much of them. Through this, Cunningham instilled a confidence and professionalism in his fleet that stood it in good stead during the hard months that lay ahead. During the Second Sirte campaign, Cunningham was frustrated that he couldn't put to sea and lead the fleet in person. Fortunately, in R. Adm. Sir Philip Vian, he had an extremely able deputy, who was by then something of an expert in Malta convoy operations. Given the odds, this campaign would fully test the abilities and resolve of both Cunningham and Vian.

Like Cunningham, **Rear Admiral Sir Philip Vian** (1894–1968) had earned a reputation as a 'destroyer man' and was groomed for higher things after commanding a destroyer flotilla during the inter-war years. Vian was born in London and schooled at Osborne, before becoming a naval cadet in 1907, at the age of 13. During World War I, he participated in the Battle of Jutland while serving on board a destroyer, before specializing as a gunnery officer. In 1933, he was given command of the destroyer HMS *Active*, and in 1935, after his promotion to captain, Vian commanded a destroyer flotilla in the Mediterranean.

When World War II began, Vian was commanding another flotilla in home waters. In 1940, as captain of the flotilla leader HMS *Cossack*, he played a leading part in the capture of the German supply ship *Altmark*, following a boarding action in Norwegian waters. Vian was awarded a Distinguished Service Order (DSO) for this successful and much-publicized action. The following year, Vian's destroyers attacked the German battleship

Bismarck. Vian made flag rank the following year, and in October 1941 was given command of the 15th Cruiser Squadron in the Mediterranean, flying his flag in *Naiad* and then *Cleopatra*. It was in this capacity that he took charge of the Covering Force for MW-10, the next fast convoy to Malta.

Cunningham described Vian as 'the most brilliant and capable officer' in his command. Vian certainly had the ability to draw excellence from his subordinates through a combination of encouragement and training. During his time as commander of the cruiser squadron, Vian had built up a friendship with his warship commanders, much like Nelson's famous 'band of brothers'. As a result, following thorough pre-operation discussions, all of his leading subordinates knew exactly what was expected of them. This relationship had been honed at First Sirte and during the convoy actions that followed. During the battle in March 1942, Vian's style of leadership would pay dividends. His complex manoeuvres would have been impossible were it not for this bond. Vian was also equally able to rely on his warship captains, whatever the odds they faced.

THE REGIA MARINA

In the Italian navy, Cunningham's counterpart and Vian's opponent during the battle was the same person. **Ammiraglio designato d'Armata (Acting Admiral) Angelo Iachino** (1889–1976) was both the commander of the Italian fleet based in Taranto and the battlefleet commander when it put to sea in the operation that resulted in the Second Battle of Sirte. Iachino, who was sometimes known as 'Jachino', took over as Commander-in-Chief of the Squadra Navale in early December 1940, and remained in command of the navy's main striking arm until April 1943.

Ammiraglio designato d'Armata (Acting Admiral) Angelo Iachino, pictured on the bridge of his flagship *Littorio*, accompanied by a signalman and a lookout. As he had been during the Battle of Matapan a year before, Iachino was encumbered by risk-averse orders from the Supermarina, the Italian navy's high command.

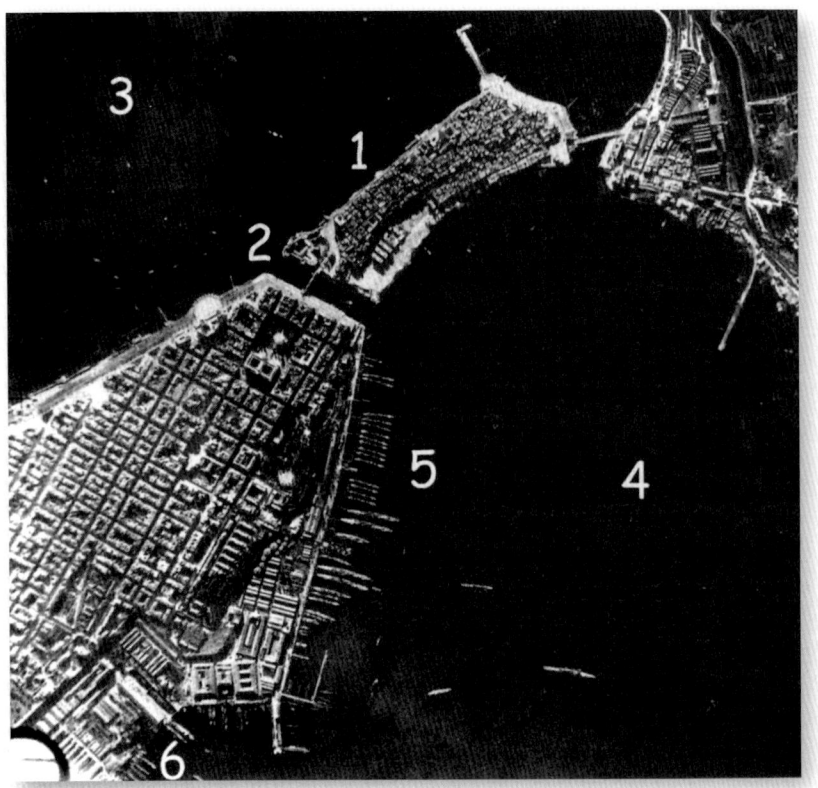

A British aerial reconnaissance photograph of the Italian port of Naples, home of Adm. Iachino's battlefleet, the Squadra Navale. Its main anchorage was at (3), in the Mar Grande, while smaller vessels used the Mar Piccolo (5). Taranto's proximity to the convoy route from Alexandria to Malta made it the most important Italian naval base of the war. It was also the departure point for many of the Axis convoys bound for Libya.

Iachino was a native of Sanremo in Liguria, on the Mediterranean coast of northern Italy. Despite being the son of a schoolteacher, the youth decided on a naval career and so in 1904, when he was 15, he became a cadet at the naval academy at Livorno. He served during the Italo-Turkish War of 1911–12, and by the time Italy entered World War I in 1915, Iachino was a *tenente* (lieutenant), serving in the dreadnought *Giulio Cesare*. Then, in 1917, he was given his first command, a torpedo boat, *PN-66*, which was stationed in the Adriatic. He briefly saw action off Pola, and was presented with a medal for valour.

During the 1920s, Iachino served as a naval attaché to the Italian embassy in China and then commanded the gunboat *Ermanno Carlotto* based in the Italian colony of Tientsin (Tienjin), near Peking. In 1928, as a *capitano di fregata* (commander), Iachino was given command of a destroyer, followed by the light cruiser *Armando Diaz* after his promotion. In 1938 he reached flag rank, becoming an *ammiraglio di divisione* (rear admiral), and held an operational command in the western Mediterranean, supervising Italian blockading operations during the Spanish Civil War. In 1939, Iachino was promoted to the rank of *ammiraglio di squadra* (vice admiral), and when Italy entered the war in June 1940 he was given command of the 2nd Naval Squadron, a mixed force of cruisers and destroyers.

He participated in the Battle of Spartivento in November 1940, and in its aftermath he replaced the battlefleet (Squadra Navale) commander Ammiraglio Campioni. It was at this point that he was awarded the rank of *ammiraglio designato d'armata*, an acting admiral's position, for which there was no equivalent outside the Regia Marina. As a battlefleet commander, Iachino was limited by the damage inflicted on his six capital ships at Taranto in November 1940. As a result, the following April, when he led his battlefleet to sea on the operation towards Crete that resulted in the Battle of Matapan, Iachino only had one operational battleship at his disposal.

Although a skilled naval commander, Iachino had been hampered at Matapan by restrictive orders from the Supermarina – the Italian navy's high command – which were the result of Mussolini's determination not to risk his battlefleet unnecessarily. During the battles of First Sirte and Second Sirte, Iachino was forced to operate under even more restrictive orders. It was these that forced him to break off the action in December, and to avoid unnecessary risk the following March. It would be interesting to know how

Iachino might have fought the battle if these restrictions had been lifted. From his memoirs, there is a suggestion that he might have been considerably more aggressive.

The first contact with R. Adm. Vian's Covering Force at Second Sirte was made by **Ammiraglio di Divisione Angelo Parona** (1889–1977) and his cruiser force. Parona was from Novara in Piedmont, in the north-west of Italy, and in 1907, like Iachino, he became a cadet in the naval academy in Livorno. During the Italo-Turkish War, he served on board the cruiser *Varese*, which saw some action off the Libyan coast. By Italy's entry into World War I, Parona was a *tenente*, serving in the obsolete battleship *Sardegna*, flagship of the naval forces defending Venice. Parona, though, served ashore with a naval brigade, and saw extensive action on the Isonzo front.

In 1917, he was given command of the submarine *F-17* and distinguished himself during the naval campaign against Austria-Hungary in the Adriatic. After the war, he stayed in the submarine arm of the fleet, and by 1927, as *capitano di fregata*, he was given command of a submarine flotilla. A staff appointment followed, when he translated a German treatise on U-boat operations into Italian. He reached the rank of *capitano di vascello* in 1932, and after two years as a naval attaché in Paris, Parona was given command of the cruiser *Trieste*. In 1938, he reached flag rank and was given another staff post ashore. His real talents, though, lay in submarines, and so in 1940 Parona was given command of Italy's submarine forces operating in the Atlantic, which were based in Bordeaux.

He learned from the Germans and greatly improved the efficiency of the Italian submarine forces. In April 1941, Parona was promoted to *ammiraglio di squadra*, but after many of his boats were recalled to the Mediterranean he was considered too high-ranking to continue in his post. So, in November, he was given command of the 3rd Cruiser Division (3ª Divisione Incrociatori), flying his flag in *Gorizia*. It was in this capacity that he participated in both the First and the Second Battle of Sirte. As a submarine commander, Parona had distinguished himself as both courageous and aggressive. However, like Iachino, he was forced to operate under incredibly restrictive orders, which gave him no leeway to show just how capable a commander he could be. Like Iachino, Parona was capable and widely respected, yet essentially both men were forced to fight a battle with one hand tied behind their backs – constrained from delivering a decisive blow against the enemy by the caution of their superiors.

Ammiraglio di Squadra (Vice Admiral) Angelo Parona (right) commanded the Italian submarine force operating in the Atlantic, before being given command of the 3rd Naval Division, based in Messina. Here, Parona is pictured with Vizeadmiral Karl Dönitz, the commander of Germany's U-boat fleet.

OPPOSING FORCES

THE ROYAL NAVY

The MW-10 convoy operation was carried out at a time when the Royal Navy's Mediterranean Fleet was at its lowest ebb. In March 1942, Adm. Cunningham had no aircraft carriers, battleships or even heavy cruisers at his disposal. As a result, the Regia Marina could deploy an overwhelming superior force in any surface action. So, Cunningham had to rely on his light cruisers and destroyers to escort this vital Malta convoy, supported by whatever aircraft the RAF could provide. Even these cruisers were not from the most powerful classes, such as the Town or Colony classes with their dozen 6in guns. Instead, R. Adm. Vian's Covering Force consisted of smaller Dido-class anti-aircraft (AA) cruisers. However, they were armed with a modern dual-purpose gun, the 5.25in (13.3cm) Quick-Firing Mark III. Vian's flagship *Cleopatra* and its sister ships *Dido* and *Euryalus* mounted ten of these power-loaded semi-automatic guns, in five twin turrets. These were capable of surface use as well as anti-aircraft fire, and were fast-firing.

These guns were also provided with a fire control radar and linked to an air early warning radar. In their anti-aircraft role, especially when working in pairs, these cruisers could put up a heavy anti-aircraft barrage, which acted as a real deterrent to enemy bombers. They fired an 80lb (36.3kg) semi armour-piercing or high-explosive shell, with an anti-aircraft ceiling of 46,500ft (14,170m) at 70° elevation, and with a rate of fire of 8rpm this heavy barrage could be maintained for the duration of most air attacks. For surface combat, the same dual-purpose gun had an effective range of 13,000yds (6½ miles). Again, radar fire control improved the accuracy of firing in surface as well as anti-aircraft actions. At that range, their shells could penetrate up to 2½in of armour, which made them a threat to *Trento*, *Bande Nere* and the destroyers, but not to the better-armoured *Gorizia*. The maximum range of the gun was

Throughout 1941, Adm. Cunningham possessed a powerful battle squadron, which he used with great effect off Cape Matapan that March. However, one by one these battleships were lost; of the three shown here, *Barham* (front) was sunk by *U-331* in November, while the following month *Queen Elizabeth* (centre) and *Valiant* (background) were both seriously damaged in an Italian midget submarine attack. Without a battlefleet, Cunningham had to rely on Vian's cruisers to support his fast convoys sailing between Alexandria and Malta.

The stylish Italian light cruiser *Giovanni delle Bande Nere*, one of four ships of the first group of Condottieri-class cruisers, pictured shortly before the war. *Bande Nere* was fast, capable of making over 36kts, but this was achieved by reducing the cruiser's armoured protection to a minimum.

around 24,000yds (21,945m), or 12 sea miles. This came as a surprise to the Italians, as the guns had a longer range than they expected.

The fourth cruiser, *Penelope*, the sole cruiser survivor of Malta's Force K, was a small light cruiser, armed with six 6in/50 (15.2cm) Mark XXIII guns. These fired a 112lb (50.8kg) shell and had a maximum range of around 12 miles. Essentially, they were broadly similar to the guns of the Italian light cruiser *Bande Nere*, except after months of action raiding Italian convoy routes, the crew of *Penelope* were highly experienced. Also, by temporarily switching to manual loading, these guns could increase their rate of fire from around 6 to 8 rounds a minute (rpm) – until the gunners grew too tired to continue. All of these cruisers also mounted 2pdr (40mm) 'pom-poms' as close-range anti-aircraft weapons and were fitted with 21in (53.3cm) torpedo tubes – six torpedoes in two triple launchers. Unlike the Italian cruisers, none of these British ones carried floatplanes. So, Vian lacked the dedicated air reconnaissance capability that was available to his Italian counterpart.

One of the big advantages Vian had, though, was the experience of his commanders. Like many of their crew, Capt. Bush of *Euryalus*, Grantham of *Cleopatra* and McCall of *Dido* had either commanded Dido-class cruisers before or had acquired extensive experience in the Mediterranean during the evacuation of Crete and the resupply of Tobruk. The same could be said of the destroyer flotilla commanders, and most of the individual destroyer captains and crew too. Of these destroyers, the two Tribal class ones, *Sikh* and *Zulu*, were designed for surface action and mounted eight 4.7in (12cm) guns apiece. The same weapon was mounted in the smaller J, K & N-class and L & M-class destroyers, which made up the rest of the two flotillas under Vian's command. Their main offensive weapon was their 21in (53.3cm) Mark IX torpedoes, which had a range of up to 7 miles, running at 30kts, but obviously the chance of achieving a hit was greatly enhanced if launched at a much shorter range.

Vian knew his ship captains and their crews knew their job. In the wartime Royal Navy, thorough professionalism was virtually taken for granted. However, it was Vian who turned the 15th Cruiser Squadron into a crack formation through repeated training, the conducting of offensive sweeps and the passing on of his own tactical demands and doctrines. Even before the convoy operation began, on 15 March he sent *Dido* and *Euryalus* off to bombard Rhodes, accompanied by six destroyers. As the squadron had just lost *Naiad*, Vian's old flagship, this was Vian's way of keeping his men

Capt. Eric Bush, commander of HMS *Euryalus*, turns to face the photographer as his cruiser escorts Convoy MW-10 towards Malta as they pass through Bomb Alley on 21 March. The cruiser's guns are at maximum elevation in anticipation of an air attack.

from dwelling on setbacks. His counter to the loss was, in his words, 'a bit of offensive action'. This thorough training meant that when the convoy was attacked, the men of Vian's Covering Force knew exactly what to do when encountering the enemy. Vian had successfully welded them into a highly efficient force, thoroughly versed in his own tactics and wishes.

THE REGIA MARINA

Adm. Angelo Iachino had a powerful, thoroughly modern force at his disposal, though it was one with limitations. At its core was the battleship *Littorio*, namesake of its three-ship class, and the flagship of his battlefleet. *Littorio* had been completed a month before Italy entered the war. Two sister ships, *Vittorio Veneto* and *Roma*, were completed in April 1940 and June 1942, respectively. A fourth battleship, *Impero*, was launched in 1939, but was never completed due to wartime pressure on Italy's shipyards. The Regia Marina's four other battleships had all been built before World War I and had subsequently been modernized. The Littorio class had been designed during the 1930s, drawing on the latest advances in capital ship design and protection. Originally, it was hoped that the class would carry 16in (40.6cm) guns, but this scheme was abandoned as the time and cost of their development would be prohibitive. Instead, a 15in (38.1cm) gun was mounted as it had already been partly developed.

Littorio mounted nine Italian-built 15in/50 (38.1cm) Model 1934 guns in three triple turrets – two forward and one aft. These guns were more powerful and had a longer range than their older British counterparts. They fired armour-piercing or semi armour-piercing shells weighing 1,952lb (884.8kg), which, at maximum elevation, had a range of up to 23 miles. The problem was shell quality, which sometimes produced erratic effects, with

The Italian heavy cruiser *Trento* pictured in Messina, shortly after the battle. Trento formed part of V. Adm. Parona's 3rd Cruiser Division, which sailed from Messina to rendezvous with Iachino's flagship in the Ionian Sea. During the battle, *Trento* fired 355 20.3cm (8in) shells, but no direct hits were achieved. However, the destroyer HMS *Legion* suffered light damage from a near miss.

shells falling short or salvos being too widely spaced. After the war, Iachino blamed this on the manufacturers, who produced shells of very variable quality. *Littorio* also mounted a secondary battery of 6in (15.2cm) guns, which had a range of 13½ miles, as well as a mixed AA defence of 9cm, 37mm and 20mm guns.

As a modern battleship, *Littorio* benefited from a more advanced propulsion system than British battleships, and had a top speed of 30kts, some 5kts faster than its British counterparts. The Italian battleship had a conventional level of protection, with a 28cm (11in) armoured belt, with 35cm (13.7in) armour around the turrets and barbettes. In effect, *Littorio* had a marginal edge over the older British capital ships. The Pugliese system of anti-torpedo bulges that provided underwater protection had been much vaunted before the war. In reality, it was only marginally more efficient than other forms of inter-war anti-torpedo protective systems. However, all this was immaterial given that at Second Sirte, the British had nothing to match *Littorio*, at least in terms of firepower and protection. The only threat they posed to Iachino's flagship was from a successful torpedo attack. When that came, Iachino wisely broke off the action.

The second component of the Italian battlefleet at Second Sirte was V. Adm. Parona's cruiser division. Both his flagship *Gorizia* and the accompanying *Trento* were heavy cruisers, each armed with eight 8in (20.3cm) guns in four twin turrets. *Trento* mounted the Model 1924 version of the gun while *Gorizia* carried the Model 1929, but, essentially, they were the same – the only thing that differed was the way the guns were mounted, although the later version was slightly more powerful. They fired a 276.2lb (125.3kg) armour-piercing shell, with a maximum range of 17 miles. However, accuracy was reduced by the poor quality of the optical rangefinders used for ranging and by the wide dispersal of the salvos. Still, at Second Sirte, they had a greater range and hitting power than anything available to the British.

The light cruiser *Bande Nere*, the third member of Parona's squadron, mounted eight 6in (15.2cm)/53 Model 1926 guns in four twin turrets. Produced by Ansaldo, the engineering company based in Genoa, these were reliable guns, firing a 110lb (50kg) armour-piercing shell with a maximum range of 12 miles. These mounts were criticized for the wide dispersal of their shell salvos and the complex loading process involved in operating them. Still, during the battle, *Banda Nere*'s guns proved the most effective in Parona's squadron. All of the cruisers also carried mixed anti-aircraft batteries of 10cm (3.7in) and 37mm anti-aircraft guns and 13.2mm anti-aircraft machine

An Italian SM.79 Sparviero ('Sparrowhawk'), pictured after carrying out an attack. These bombers, the real workhorse of the Regia Aeronautica during the Mediterranean campaign, were capable of operating as either torpedo bombers or conventional ones.

guns. Aircraft, though, were not a threat during this engagement, so they were not used. Similarly, although *Trento* and *Bande Nere* carried torpedoes, these weapons were never launched.

Another wasted resource at Second Sirte were the Soldati-class destroyers accompanying both the battleship and the cruiser division. During the action, *Ascari*, *Aviere*, *Alpino*, *Bersagliere*, *Fuciliere* and *Lanciere* were held back from the fight. Their high speed of 34kts and their main armament of 4.7in (12cm) guns and 21in torpedoes could have made a difference if they had been unleashed on the British convoy. Iachino, though, preferred to have them escort his larger warships in case of an unexpected attack. Even then, when British destroyers launched a long-range torpedo attack on *Littorio*, the destroyers were kept safely out of harm's way. Part of the reason for this was that when the attack came, it was almost nightfall. After Matapan, Iachino was painfully aware that the British warships had radar, and his ships lacked it. So, he had no wish to risk his fleet in a night action, in which the use of radar could prove decisive.

One thing working in Iachino's favour was that he and his crews had recognized the flaws in their doctrine, which had been exposed at Matapan. Over the previous 11 months, they had worked hard to either overcome them or to change their tactics to avoid repeating the same mistakes. Avoiding night action was one of these tactical changes. So too was the improvement of relations with the Regia Aeronautica, which provided some form of aerial reconnaissance for the battlefleet. This new inter-service relationship was still in its infancy, and most Italian air crews hadn't received specialist training in maritime reconnaissance or warship identification. As if to make up for it, Iachino, a gunnery expert, had worked hard to make his ships more proficient in surface combat and to overcome technical problems that limited the effectiveness of Italian gunnery and fire control. By March 1942, he was able to put to sea with the reasonable expectation that if the enemy was encountered, then his fleet would perform well enough.

The other key weapon in the Italian arsenal was aircraft. *Littorio* and all three cruisers carried floatplanes, which could be launched from a catapult if the conditions were right and used to scout out the enemy, or to act as spotter planes during gunnery engagements. It was an Ro.43 floatplane from Parona's cruisers that located the convoy and its Covering Force shortly before the battle got under way. However, the deteriorating weather conditions that day made the launching and recovery of these aircraft impractical, and so they played no further part in the battle. However, throughout 22 March, the British convoy was under near-continuous air attack from Axis air formations: Fliegerkorps X based in Greece (Eleusis near Athens), Crete (Heraklion) and Cyrenaica (Benghazi), and Fliegerkorps II operating from Sicily.

The principal attacking formation during the battle was I/Kampfgeschwader 54 (I./KG 54), based near Benghazi, which was equipped with Junkers Ju 88 twin-engined bombers. Ju 87 Stuka dive bombers from Sturzkampfgeschwader 3 based in Derna in Cyrenaicia also took part in attacks on the convoy on 22 March. The Regia Aeronautica added its weight, with SM.79 squadrons from 2° Stormo ('Wing') launching attacks on the convoy from airfields near in Benghazi. For the most part, these Axis bomber crews were not specialists in maritime strikes. So, their attacks during the operation, while courageously pursued, were ineffective. By contrast, the bombers of Fliegerkorps II were well versed in naval strikes, and their attacks on the convoy on 23 March proved the worth of this specialist training.

ORDERS OF BATTLE

ROYAL NAVY
15th Cruiser Squadron (R. Adm. Vian) [4 AA cruisers]
  Cleopatra (flagship), *Dido*, *Euryalus* (Dido-class AA cruisers); *Carlisle* (C-class light AA cruiser)
14th Destroyer Flotilla (Capt. Poland) [4 destroyers]
  Jervis (leader), *Kelvin*, *Kingston*, *Kipling* (J, K & N-class destroyers)
22nd Destroyer Flotilla (Capt. Micklethwait) [6 destroyers]
  Sikh (leader), *Zulu* (Tribal-class destroyers); *Hasty*, *Havock*, *Hero* (G, H & I-class destroyers);
  Lively (L & M-class destroyer)
5th Destroyer Flotilla (Cdr Jellicoe) [7 escort destroyers]
  Southwold (leader), *Avon Vale*, *Beaufort*, *Dulverton*, *Eridge*, *Heythrop*, *Hurworth* (Hunt-class escort destroyers)
Force K (Capt. Nicholl) [1 light cruiser, 1 destroyer]
  Penelope (flag, Arethusa-class light cruiser); *Legion* (L & M-class destroyer)
Convoy MW-10 (Convoy Commodore: Capt. Hutchinson) [4 merchant ships]
  HMS *Breconshire* (commodore's flag), SS *Clan Campbell*, MV *Pampas*, M/S *Talabot* (Norwegian)

REGIA MARINA

1st Division (Adm. Iachino)
Battleship Division (Adm. Iachino)
  Littorio (flag, Littorio-class battleship)
11th Destroyer Flotilla
  Ascari, *Aviere* (Soldati-class destroyers); *Alfredo Oriani* (Oriani-class destroyer); *Grecale* (Maestrale-class destroyer)

2nd Division (V. Adm. Parona)
3rd Cruiser Division (V. Adm. Parona)
  Gorizia (flag, Zara-class heavy cruiser); *Trento* (Trento-class heavy cruiser); *Giovanni delle Bande Nere* (Condottieri-class light cruiser)
13th Destroyer Flotilla
  Alpino, *Bersagliere*, *Fuciliere*, *Lanciere* (Soldati-class destroyers)
  Attached submarine (1): *Platino*

OPPOSING PLANS

THE ROYAL NAVY

By March 1942, it was clear that the supply situation in Malta was becoming critical. Cunningham had sent several fast supply ships from Alexandria to Malta, but it wasn't enough. He understood that he and his fleet had three main tasks: the support of the 8th Army in North Africa, the cutting of Italian supply routes between Italy and Libya and the resupply of Malta. Rommel's recent counter-attack had made all three tasks much harder. With the 8th Army grouped around Gazala, to the west of Tobruk, most of the airfields in Cyrenaica were in Axis hands. The nearest British airfield to Malta was more than 500 miles away. Bomb Alley between Cyrenaica and Crete was dominated by the Axis, making the safe transit of Cunningham's ships through those seas particularly fraught. However, Malta still needed supplies, and the flow of Axis supplies to North Africa needed to be slowed, regardless of the risk.

A brief glance at the chart revealed the basics of the situation. If a well-escorted fast convoy from Alexandria were to reach Malta, it faced a passage of some 900 miles. Given a typical convoy speed of around 12–13kts, then the voyage should take just over three days, with a daily progress of around 300 miles. So, the passage could be divided into three daily segments: D-Day ('Departure Day'), D+1 and D+2. It would leave Alexandria on D-Day, in this case Friday 20 March, and would reach Malta on D+3, during the morning of Monday 23 March. At that time of year, there were roughly equal hours of daylight and darkness. The risk of an attack at night was low. The problem, then, was to make sure the convoy made it safely through the hours of daylight.

Each 300-mile segment, 'D', 'D+1' and 'D+2', presented its own challenges. On the first, to be covered on Friday 20 March (D-Day), the main risk was from Axis submarines, and from enemy bombers operating from Crete. If the convoy left Alexandria in mid-morning, then darkness would fall as it reached longitude 28° East, which ran between Rhodes and the Egyptian coast, midway between Alexandria and the Egyptian border. So, fighter cover would be provided throughout the daylight hours of D-Day, and an anti-submarine sweep would be conducted along the Egyptian coast.

Dawn on Saturday 21 March (D+1) should find the convoy at around 25° East, which ran from Heraklion in Crete to the Libyan coast between Bardia (Bardiyeh) and Tobruk. This was the heart of Bomb Alley, and air attacks

HMS *Jervis*, commanded by Capt. Albert Poland, was the flotilla leader of the Mediterranean Fleet's 14th Destroyer Flotilla based in Alexandria. During the battle *Jervis*, pictured here later in the war, would lead the flotilla in a daring torpedo attack against the Italian battleship *Littorio*.

could be expected from both Crete and Cyrenaica. Once again, the convoy would be well protected by RAF fighters operating from North African airfields. Darkness would find it at the longitude of 23° East, which ran between the south-eastern Peloponnese in Greece and the Cyrenaican coast a little east of Derna. The darkness should shield the convoy as it passed the 'hump' of Cyrenaica.

The real danger came during the daylight hours of Sunday 22 March (D+2). By this stage, the convoy and its Covering Force would be beyond the reach of British fighters based both in North Africa and Malta. The convoy would be passing to the north of the Gulf of Sirte, and so was still within range of Axis aircraft based in Cyrenaica and southern Italy. It would also be on D+2 that the convoy would be at risk of a surface attack from the Italian battlefleet based in Taranto. This would be the most dangerous phase of the voyage. All Vian could really do was keep the convoy as far south as he could to increase the distance between it and Taranto. Too far south though and this would delay the arrival of the convoy in Malta. If it was too late then it would be left exposed to enemy air attack as the merchant ships approached the island on the morning of Monday 23 March.

To some extent, this exposure to enemy air attacks was inevitable as Vian's Covering Force – his cruisers and destroyers – were scheduled to return to Alexandria during the night of 22/23 March. Vian had scheduled their reversal of course at around 2100hrs on Sunday evening, when the convoy was expected to be passing the longitude of 17° East. That meant the convoy had to make the last 130 miles of the voyage on its own – a voyage that would take around 11 hours. With sunrise on Monday morning coming at 0600hrs, if they were up early enough the enemy airmen had two hours of daylight to attack the convoy. So, to reduce the risk, the convoy's Close Escort of seven Hunt-class escort destroyers would accompany the four merchantmen into Malta. It was also expected that from dawn onwards, air cover would be provided by fighters from RAF Malta Command.

To improve the convoy's chances, Cunningham added a few other touches to the plan. Force K, which by mid-March was reduced to just two warships, the light cruiser *Penelope* and the destroyer *Legion*, under the command of Capt. Nicholl of *Penelope*, would sail from Malta under cover of darkness on Saturday evening and rendezvous with Vian on Sunday morning. They would bolster Vian's force during those crucial hours of daylight on 22 March.

For much of 1941, and again after Rommel's surprise offensive in January 1942, the destroyers of the Mediterranean Fleet were called upon to make the 'Tobruk Run' – the ferrying of supplies from Alexandria to Malta, usually under cover of darkness. This drew the attention of German U-boats, which in turn led to the deployment of Cdr Jellicoe's 5th Destroyer Flotilla to hunt for lurking U-boats which might pose a threat to the convoy as it passed.

Then they would return to Alexandria with him – the risk of damage to them in Malta had now become too great. Although Vian and the convoy would be too far away from Malta to expect fighter air cover that Sunday, RAF Malta was asked to have a force of long-range bombers on standby to launch a strike against the Italian battlefleet if it was spotted by Vian's ships.

The other strand in Cunningham and Vian's plan was to launch a series of diversionary attacks on Axis airfields in Cyrenaica to reduce the risk of air attacks on the convoy. These would be carried out by the 8th Army's Long Range Desert Group attacking the airfields from the desert. This, it was hoped, would act as a distraction, and so reduce the number of aircraft the enemy could use to attack the convoy. In addition, RAF Egypt command was asked to launch bombing raids on the airfields at dawn on 21 and 22 March to augment these land-based attacks. These RAF air attacks would be supplemented by a Fleet Air Arm formation, 826 Naval Air Squadron (NAS), which was temporarily based ashore near Alexandria. Its Swordfish and Albacores were scheduled to bomb the Axis at Derna during the nights of 20/21 and 21/22 March.

As for the Italian fleet, a screen of British submarines would be stationed in the Gulf of Taranto and the Strait of Messina, to forewarn Vian if the Italian battlefleet put to sea. In addition, RAF Malta would use Naval Cooperation Group 201 to conduct reconnaissance flights over the central Mediterranean east of Malta, just in case the Italians slipped past the submarines. Finally, Force H, based in Gibraltar, had scheduled a 'Club Run' – the flying-off of RAF fighters from British aircraft carriers, which would then fly on to Malta. This was timed to coincide with the voyage of Vian's convoy. Ideally, this would fully occupy the Axis air units based in Sicily, making it less likely they would be free to attack the convoy as it made its final approach to Malta on Monday morning. The whole plan was well thought out and gave the fast convoy the best chance of success. In war, though, nothing is certain, and Vian stood ready to improvise the plan during the operation, if the need arose.

THE REGIA MARINA

By contrast, the Italian plan was relatively simple. The first element was intelligence gathering. The Axis maintained spy rings in both Alexandria and Malta, and so the Supermarina could, with some certainty, know when a convoy or group of warships were preparing to sail. This was augmented by sighting reports from German U-boats and Axis submarines patrolling the eastern Mediterranean, between Tobruk and Alexandria. These, at least in the case of the Germans, involved a convoluted reporting route, which delayed the receipt of any sighting reports in the Supermarina headquarters in Rome.

Even without any intelligence reports, the Axis flew regular maritime reconnaissance patrols over the eastern Mediterranean, from airfields in Crete

A rare but grainy photograph of an Italian SM.79 'Sparviero' medium bomber, in the process of dropping a torpedo during an attack on HMS *Barham* in early 1940. The Regia Aeronautica selected bomber squadrons for maritime attack duties, and converted dozens of bombers to carry torpedoes. In this instance, though, *Barham* emerged unscathed.

and Cyrenaica. If a British convoy was known to have set sail, then these were markedly increased. Once the Supermarina had a definitive sighting report of a convoy and its Close Escort, then Adm. Iachino in Taranto would be informed, and kept updated on the convoy's progress. While the bulk of the battlefleet was based at Taranto, some 350 miles north of the likely convoy route, other warships based at Brindisi at the mouth of the Aegean Sea could also be used. After sailing from Taranto, the Italian battlefleet could be astride the convoy route within 14 hours. Ideally, this would be timed to take place at dawn.

In addition, when a British convoy reached the waters between Crete and Tobruk it would enter Bomb Alley. The likelihood was that while traversing Bomb Alley, a British convoy would pass within 100 miles of the North African coast. This meant that if these attacks were well coordinated, then relays of bombers could be sent from airfields in Cyrenaica, around 40 minutes flying time away from the convoy's path. In 12 hours of daylight, multiple attacks could be made by the same bomber formations.

If the convoy came within 100 miles of Malta, this also put it well within range of Axis airfields in southern Italy and Sicily. So, Fliegerkorps II formations, which, together with Regia Aeronautica units, were already heavily committed to the bombing offensive against Malta, could be diverted to attack the convoy from the north and north-west. This was particularly useful, as both the Germans and the Italians maintained bomber squadrons there that were specially trained in maritime strikes. It was these which were earmarked to prey on the convoy as it made its final approach to Malta. In addition, when a British convoy drew close to Malta, other Axis bombers would concentrate on the RAF airfields in Malta, to neutralize any attempt to provide air cover for the convoy during its final approach to the island.

Once the Italian battlefleet put to sea, Iachino planned to use his flagship *Littorio* as the main striking force, as it had the firepower to keep the enemy lighter forces at bay as it sought out the convoy. The cruiser force and its attached destroyers would range ahead of the battleship, and attempt to locate the convoy and its Covering Force. V. Adm. Parona, commanding Iachino's cruisers, was under strict orders not to be drawn into a fight with the enemy. His job was to locate the British and then rendezvous with *Littorio*. Then, the combined Italian force would use its superior speed compared to the convoy to work its way between the convoy and Malta. After brushing off any Covering Force, and protected by the cruisers and destroyers, Iachino would use his battleship to destroy the convoy.

Iachino had already established his likely battleground – the same waters to the north of the Gulf of Sirte where he had encountered Vian during the First Battle of Sirte. Iachino expected the British to make good use of smoke to screen the convoy and to fight aggressively to prevent the Italians from reaching it. So, without radar, Iachino was dependent on his floatplanes to follow enemy movements, and on the speed of his own warships to outmanoeuvre the British, and so make contact with the convoy. It was a sound plan of operations, especially if the convoy was detected and attacked by Axis aircraft during its passage. This would give Iachino all the information he needed to ensure his battlefleet was perfectly placed to block the convoy's progress, and to destroy it.

The planned voyage of Convoy MW-10, 20–22 March

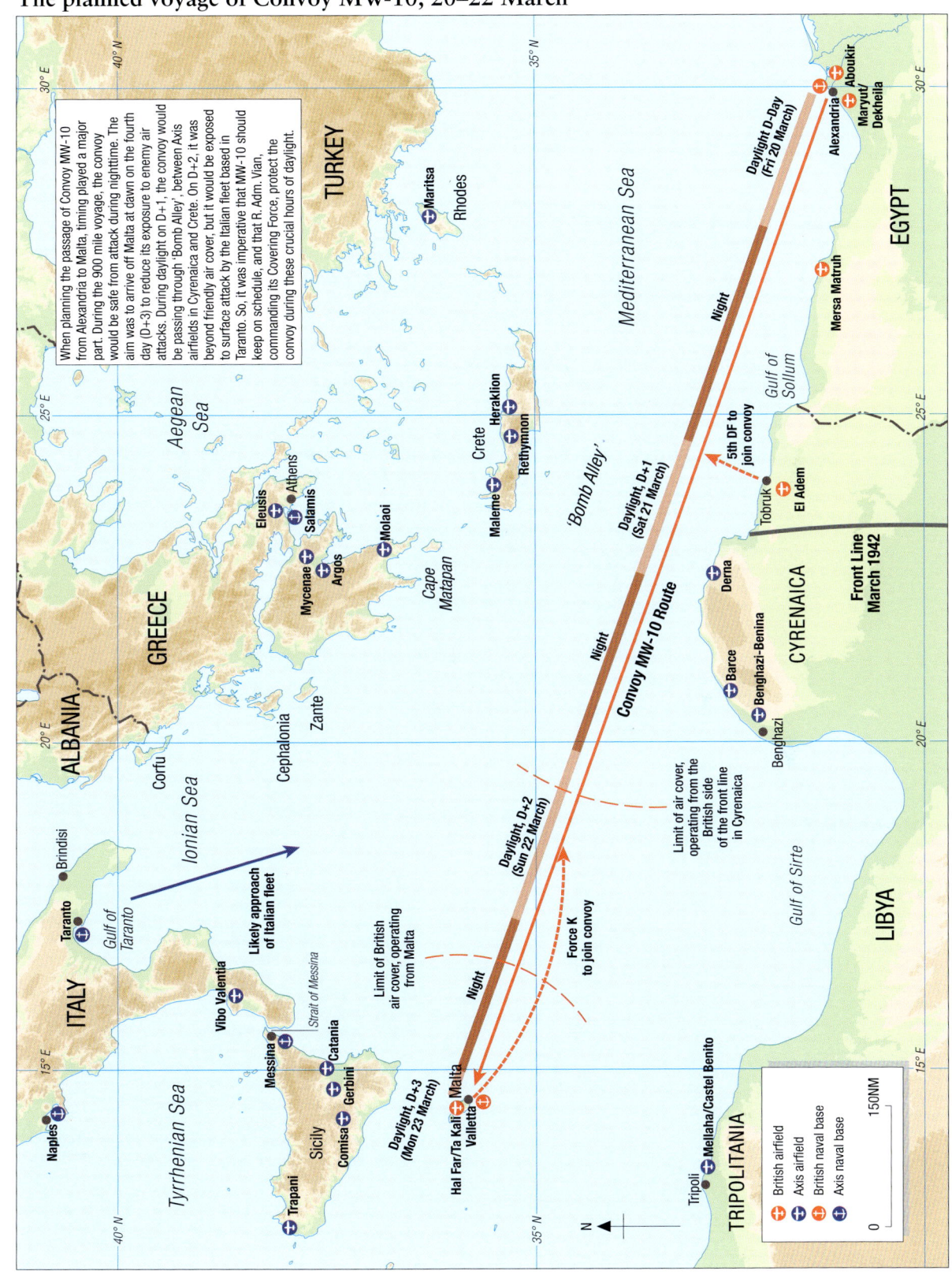

THE CAMPAIGN

OPERATION *MG-1*

The preliminaries of the operation began on the morning of Wednesday 18 March, two days before the convoy's sailing. At 0730hrs, Cdr Christopher Jellicoe's 5th Destroyer Flotilla put to sea from Alexandria for an anti-submarine sweep up the Egyptian coast, but concentrating on the Gulf of Sollum (Sallum) astride the Egyptian–Libyan border, 250 miles to the east. Capt. Lord Mountbatten's 'Fighting Fifth' flotilla had been largely destroyed during the Crete campaign the previous May, but in December it was reformed in Alexandria. In its new form, it consisted of newly built escort destroyers. These first proved their worth during the fast convoy operations of early 1942, and by mid-March, the flotilla was made up of seven Hunt-class (Type 2) vessels: Jellicoe's *Southwold*, *Avon Vale*, *Beaufort*, *Dulverton*, *Eridge*, *Heythrop* and *Hurworth*. Incidentally, Cdr Jellicoe was not directly related to Admiral the Fleet Lord Jellicoe.

Jellicoe's orders were to conduct the sweep, codenamed Operation *MG-1*, then put in to Tobruk. There the flotilla would refuel before joining

The Hunt-class (Type 2) escort destroyer HMS *Avon Vale*. *Avon Vale* formed part of the Mediterranean Fleet's 5th Destroyer Flotilla, which was given the task of forming the Close Escort of Convoy MW-10. Their powerful anti-aircraft armament proved vital in repelling the air attacks on the convoy during the battle.

Convoy MW-10 at sea around dawn on Saturday as it drew close to the port. *Beaufort*'s departure, though, was delayed due to a fouled propeller. *Beaufort* would catch up with the flotilla later. By dawn on Friday 20 March, the flotilla was 40 miles off Sidi Barrani, 200 miles west of Alexandria, at the western end of the Gulf. It was there that the sweep began in earnest. The flotilla made 14kts, zig-zagging as it went, with each escort spaced 1,500yds apart.

No contacts had been found, when, at 1055hrs, the bridge staff of HMS *Heythrop* spotted two torpedoes passing astern of them. The officer of the watch began turning the escort to starboard, when a third torpedo struck the warship's port side, near the mainmast. The explosion almost blew *Heythrop*'s stern off and the ship began listing. One of the boilers was wrecked and the other was shut down, leaving the escort destroyer wallowing helplessly. *Heythrop* was taken under tow by *Eridge*, which tried to tow it into Tobruk, escorted by *Avon Vale*. However, by 1600hrs, the stricken escort's commanding officer, Lt Cdr Robert Stafford, judged it was now hopeless, and gave the order to abandon ship. Minutes later, *Heythrop* capsized but remained afloat, forcing *Eridge* to sink the crippled escort using guns. In all, 16 of the 150-strong crew of *Heythrop* died in the attack.

The torpedoes had been fired by Oberleutnant Georg-Werner Fraatz's *U-652*, a Type VIIC U-boat. The boat had left its base on Salamis near Athens on 18 March to patrol the waters between Tobruk and Alexandria, with two other U-boats, *U-559* and *U-568*. The surfaced U-boat spotted the approaching flotilla at 1000hrs and crash dived. Fraatz let the flotilla approach him and waited until it was passing him. He then turned to face *Heythrop* and launched a spread of four torpedoes at a range of 1,000m. After one of them hit the escort destroyer, Fraatz dived to 150m before the inevitable depth-charge attack.

Southwold, *Dulverton* and *Hurworth* dropped 79 depth charges that day, but failed to damage the U-boat. At 1700hrs, the escorts withdrew towards Tobruk and *U-652* headed north towards Salamis. The 5th Flotilla reached Tobruk later that evening. The night was spent refuelling and replacing depth charges and landing the dead and wounded. Cdr Jellicoe led his remaining five Hunts to sea at 0300hrs on Saturday morning for the flotilla's rendezvous with the convoy. Still missing was *Beaufort*. Having dealt with the fouled propeller, the escort destroyer reached Tobruk that morning, after the rest of the flotilla had left. After refuelling, Lt Standish Roche took *Beaufort* out to sea again and finally rejoined the flotilla on Saturday evening.

A German Type VIIC U-boat at sea. The German decision to support the Italians by sending U-boats into the Mediterranean resulted in a number of major losses to the Royal Navy in 1941–42, including an aircraft carrier and a battleship. On the eve of the Sirte battle, *U-652* weakened the convoy's Close Escort by sinking the escort destroyer HMS *Heythrop*.

D-DAY AND D+1

At dawn on Friday 20 March, the Blue Peter flag was lowered from the mainmast of HMS *Breconshire* and the four merchant ships that made up Convoy MW-10 began raising their anchors and proceeding out of Alexandria harbour. The Convoy Commodore for this voyage was Capt. Colin Hutchinson, who commanded the auxiliary supply ship HMS *Breconshire*. Both Hutchinson and *Breconshire*, a fast Hong Kong-built merchantman, were veterans of the Malta run. The rest of the convoy was made up of SS *Clan Campbell*, MV *Pampas* and M/S *Talabot*.

At 0700hrs, they slipped passed the port's western mole, past the El Agami lighthouse, and headed towards the north-west. There, just outside the port, they were met by the light AA cruiser HMS *Carlisle*, commanded by Capt. Douglas Neame. Also waiting to accompany the convoy were the six destroyers of Capt. St John Micklethwait's 22nd Destroyer Flotilla, the flotilla leader *Sikh*, followed by *Zulu*, *Hasty*, *Havock*, *Hero* and *Lively*. Progress was set at 12kts, the speed of the slowest ship, *Clan Campbell*, the convoy and its surrounding escorts zig-zagging as they headed into the eastern Atlantic. Force B, R. Adm. Vian's Covering Force, would follow the convoy to sea later that evening.

For Capt. Hutchinson, the day passed without incident. Throughout the day's passage, the convoy was escorted by relays of RAF fighters, operating from airfields in Egypt and Cyrenaica. In fact, the Luftwaffe and Regia Aeronautica never put in an appearance, thanks largely to the scale of the air cover afforded to the convoy. At 1800hrs that evening, shortly before dark, Force B put to sea from Alexandria and began catching up with the convoy. By that stage, it was 140 miles away, about 60 miles north of the Egyptian coastal town of Marsa Matruh. Sunset came at 1835hrs, which brought the convoy a dozen hours of respite from the threat of air attack. The only real problem facing Hutchinson that evening was the poor performance of

Captain St John Micklethwait commanded the 22nd Destroyer Flotilla during the battle. His ship, the Tribal-class destroyer HMS *Sikh*, was in the thick of the fight, laying smoke to screen the convoy and even exchanging fire with the Italian battleship *Littorio*. Afterwards, Micklethwait was promoted, becoming a rear admiral.

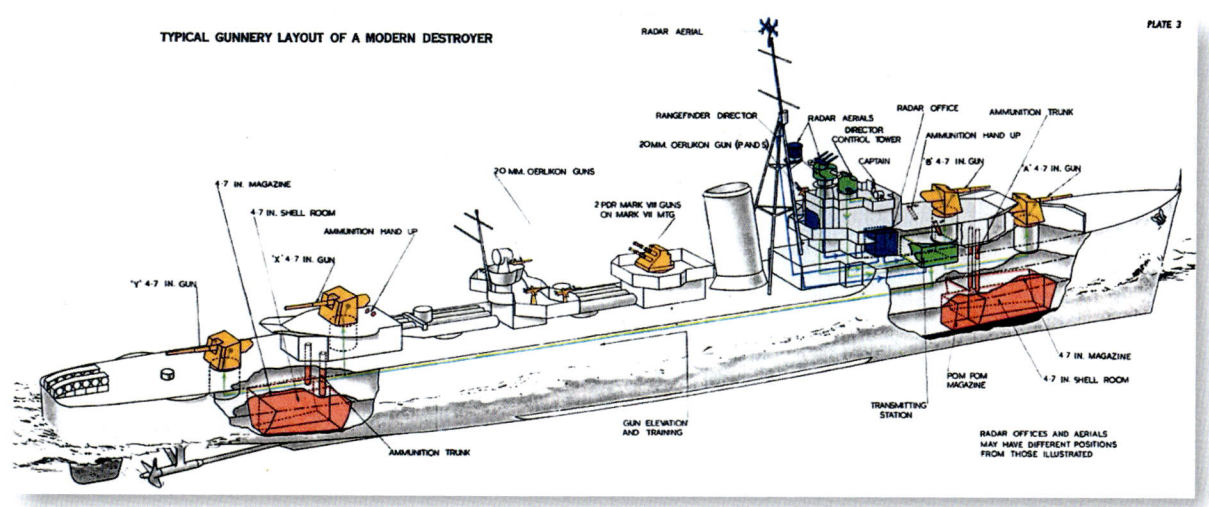

This wartime diagram shows the weapons layout of one of the Royal Navy's war-built destroyers, typical of the J, K & N or L & M classes. The four single 4.7in gun mounts were arrayed fore and aft, with two multiple torpedo launchers amidships, and a 2pdr 'pom-pom' anti-aircraft gun. By 1942 many of these destroyers had their after torpedo tube removed, and replaced by a 4in QF anti-aircraft gun. Also worth noting is the Type 286 combined air and surface warning radar set atop the foremast, mounted in all of the British destroyers in the two flotillas, apart from *Hero*, which had no radar.

SS *Clan Campbell*. It was still making 12kts, but the ship's master reported that it had engine trouble and was struggling to keep up with the convoy.

The night proved uneventful, and dawn on Saturday 21 March found the convoy to the north of the Egyptian–Libyan border. There was a slight swell, and the forecast told of gradually worsening conditions over the next few days. The wind, then blowing at 20mph from the south-west, still bore the heat of the desert when it reached the ships, 75 miles offshore. Sunrise was at 0626hrs, and the light revealed a group of warships approaching from the south-east. It was Cdr Jellicoe's 5th Flotilla. By 0730hrs, the escort destroyers had formed a protective ring around the convoy, while Micklethwait's flotilla took up station ahead and astern of the formation. Lookouts scanned the partly clouded sky, but the only aircraft to be seen were the RAF fighters, which arrived shortly after dawn and flew in a protective formation over the convoy.

What seemed surprising was the lack of any enemy aircraft. After all, dawn found them within Bomb Alley. This lack of enemy activity was largely due to the bombing raids carried out at dawn that morning by the RAF. The airfields at Barce, Bera at Benghazi, Benina and Derna were all attacked, and while physical damage was minimal, the airport operations were significantly disrupted. In addition, during the previous night (20/21 March) the Swordfish and Albacores of 826 NAS conducted a nighttime bombing raid on Derna airfield. They repeated the attack the following night (21/22 March). Again, while little physical damage was inflicted – the Italians losing a single Fiat BR.20 Cigogna bomber destroyed on the ground – the nocturnal attack appears to have been disruptive.

In addition, patrols from the Long Range Desert Group also launched raids on two of these airfields and their supply depots, causing further chaos. The group had been watching the Via Balbia road between Tripoli and Benghazi, but was still able to launch a series of small diversions around Benghazi and Barce. As a result, it appears that no maritime reconnaissance flights took off from Cyrenaican airfields on either Saturday or Sunday. As an Italian report admitted afterwards, 'Consequently, the Axis air forces in North Africa didn't conduct any reconnaissance flights at sea.' So, the convoy was able to continue its voyage unmolested.

At 1035hrs on Saturday 21 March, lookouts on HMS *Jervis*, flotilla leader of the 14th Destroyer Flotilla, sighted the convoy ahead of them, and within an hour R. Adm. Vian's Force B had joined it, taking up position 2 miles to the north of the convoy, off its starboard beam. At that moment, Force B officially became the Covering Force, charged with protecting the convoy from enemy surface attacks and augmenting its air defences. Strangely, despite being in Bomb Alley, with the convoy now directly north of Gazala, the front line in the Western Desert, the enemy reconnaissance aircraft still hadn't appeared. Even the long-range Junkers Ju 88 reconnaissance flights from the large Luftwaffe airfield at Heraklion in Crete hadn't been seen, and throughout the day, the screens of Vian's air search radar remained empty of contacts.

The only real trouble that day came from within the convoy itself. After being damaged during a previous fast-convoy run in January, SS *Clan Campbell* had been repaired in Alexandria. Still, the job had been rushed to get the freighter ready for this convoy and the engines were still problematic. During D-Day, *Clan Campbell* had struggled to keep up with the rest, even though the other three merchantmen could make more than the convoy's speed of 12kts. By late on Saturday morning, though, *Clan Campbell* reported to the Convoy Commodore that it could only make 9kts. So, the convoy slowed its pace to allow *Clan Campbell* to keep up. This would inevitably have an impact on the timing of the ships' arrival in Malta. If they arrived too late on D+3, the convoy could be torn apart by air attacks before it entered Valletta harbour.

As Capt. Hutchinson wrote later, '*Clan Campbell* could not do more than about 9 knots, whereas we should have been good for 12 knots. We were, therefore, behind time all the way.' He added, 'This had a tremendous influence on the outcome of the operation.' In fact, repairs to the freighter's engines carried out during the day allowed *Clan Campbell* to pick up speed, and by nightfall it was making 12kts again. While this was concerning for Vian, and for Cunningham back in Alexandria, the good news was that the 'Club Run' by Force H, the delivering of Spitfire fighters to Malta, appeared to have grabbed the attention of the Axis air units in Sicily. Between that, and the continued disruption caused by more RAF bombing attacks in Cyrenaica, Axis aircraft never came within sight of the convoy for most of the day.

This changed at 1700hrs on Saturday evening. By that stage, the convoy and its Covering Force were approximately 45 miles due north of Al Hamamah, the most northerly part of Cyrenaica, near Beda Littoria (Al Baydah). A few

The Fleet Air Arm's attack on Taranto on 11 November 1941 altered the course of the war in the Mediterranean. Here, the Italian battleship *Conte di Cavour* can be seen, sunk in shallow water. In all, three Italian battleships (*Conte di Cavour*, *Caio Duilio* and *Littorio*) were disabled, although the last two were repaired and returned to service in 1942.

The Dido-class AA cruiser HMS *Euryalus*, preceded by another Dido, HMS *Cleopatra*, pictured on 11 March 1942, fending off an Axis air attack during a passage from Malta to Alexandria. That same day, another Dido in the force, HMS *Naiad*, was torpedoed and sunk by *U-565*.

minutes later, a high-flying Junkers Ju 52 transport plane passed close by the convoy, en route from Derna in Cyrenaica to Heraklion in Crete. The convoy was sighted and duly reported. Then, at 1746hrs, an hour before sunset, the convoy was spotted by a patrolling Italian submarine, the *Onice*. This meant that by the evening of D+1, the enemy knew that a convoy was at sea, and so too was Vian's Covering Force. As a result, Vian expected the convoy to be subjected to heavy air attacks the following day. There was also a strong possibility that the Italian battlefleet would put to sea to intercept them at some point over the next 24 hours.

Sure enough, at 0100hrs on Sunday morning D+2 (22 March), the British submarine *P-36* sent a signal to Alexandria reporting that the Italian battlefleet had put to sea. *P-36* had been lying off Taranto, waiting for exactly that moment. Vian received the signal too but noted that it provided no details of its strength – only its course and speed, a heading of 150°, at 23kts. On board *Cleopatra*, Vian and his flag captain took a close look at the chart. The convoy was heading due west (270°) at 12kts. The Italians would be heading directly towards the convoy, or rather where it would be on Sunday afternoon, somewhere to the north of the Gulf of Sirte. He knew modern Italian warships were fast, and so they could cover the intervening 340 miles in around 12 to 13 hours. That meant that contact with the enemy could be made anytime from noon onwards. Around 1400hrs was considered the most likely time this might take place.

In fact, the increasing south-easterly wind and lumpy seas would probably slow down the Italians, particularly their destroyers, which would not cope as well in such conditions as the larger warships. So, Adm. Iachino – if he were leading the enemy force – would probably have to reduce speed. Both Vian and Capt. Grantham agreed that by turning slightly more to the south, this contact might be delayed by a few hours. That would delay contact until around 1600hrs. If that were the case, then Vian would only have to hold off the Italians until sunset, a little over two hours later. So, they decided to alter course to 250° at 0800hrs the following morning. The reason for this delay was that Vian had a rendezvous to keep earlier that Sunday morning.

At 2015hrs on Saturday evening, the Arethusa-class light cruiser HMS *Penelope* crept out of Valletta harbour and headed through the swept channel through the minefields to reach the open sea. *Penelope* and the cruiser's consort, the L & M-class destroyer HMS *Legion*, were all that remained of Force K, the Malta Strike Force. They then steamed east at 23kts, for a rendezvous with Vian at 0800hrs the following morning. This was set at position 34°10'N, 19°30'E, some 270 miles south-east of Malta. Meanwhile, the convoy continued on through the night, through an increasingly lumpy sea. At dawn, shortly after 0600hrs, the sea and sky around the convoy was clear of the enemy, and the British continued on, following their due westerly heading.

At 0725hrs, Force K was sighted to the west, and right on schedule, the rendezvous was made as Capt. Angus Nicholl of *Penelope* steamed past Vian's flagship *Cleopatra*, to take up position at the back of the Covering Force. As Nicholl recalled afterwards, 'As we met the formation on the morning of the 22nd, the *Penelope* passed close to *Cleopatra*, and I could see Vian on the bridge greeting me by making a large V sign with his arms.' The previous day, Vian had a bomber fly ahead to Malta to deliver his detailed orders to Nicholl, outlining his tactical plan in the event of an encounter with the Italian fleet. Unbeknown to Vian, it didn't reach Nicholl before *Penelope* sailed. So, both Nicholl and Cdr Richard Jessel of *Legion* had to anticipate Vian's wishes once the fighting began.

Once the rendezvous was completed, Vian ordered the convoy to alter 20° to port, onto its new course of 250°. On that course, and with the convoy making 12kts, it would pass the longitude of 18° East in six hours, at around 1400hrs. This line of longitude featured in Cunningham's instructions to Vian. These stated that if the Italian battlefleet was encountered, the Covering Force would engage it, allowing the convoy to escape. The convoy would only turn back to Alexandria if the enemy attacked to the east of this line of longitude. If to the west, then Cunningham considered it likely the convoy would make it safely into Malta, even if forced to disperse, if the enemy pushed past Vian. That longitude, 200 miles from Malta, was considered within reach of fighter cover from the island.

At 0800hrs, when the British altered course, the convoy still had fighter cover. However, these RAF aircraft were flying at the very limit of their

HMS *Cleopatra*, flagship of R. Adm. Vian's cruiser squadron, pictured at anchor in Scapa Flow shortly before the cruiser's deployment to the Mediterranean in late 1941. Radar antennas can be seen atop its mastheads, although the smaller mast rising by the forecastle belongs to another smaller vessel, lying off *Cleopatra*'s port side.

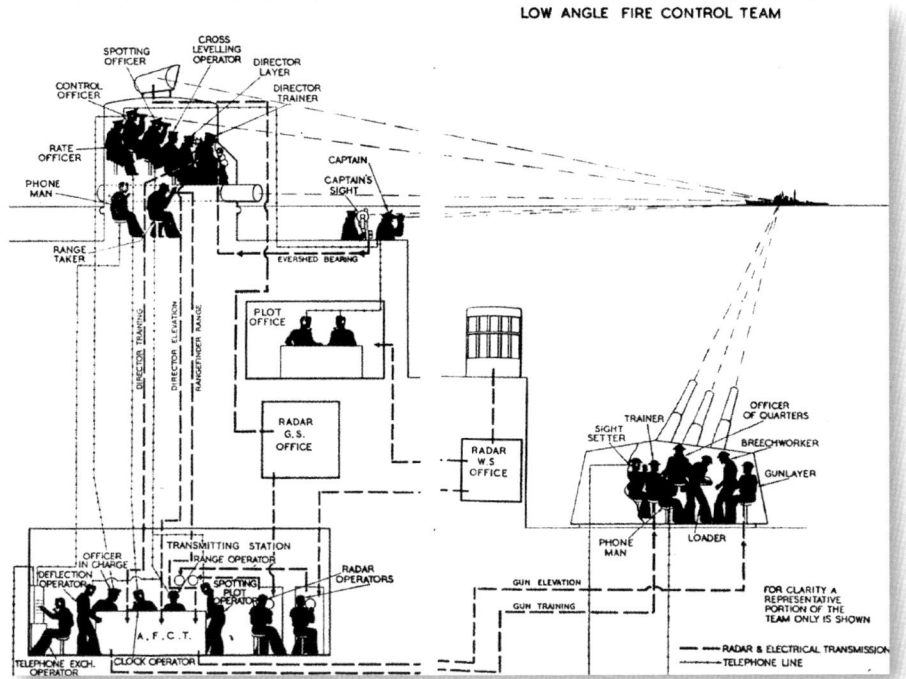

LOW ANGLE FIRE CONTROL TEAM

In 1942, the efficiency of British naval gunnery was boosted by the provision of fire control radars. These augmented visual targeting and rangefinding by the director control tower team. Both sources of information were then processed using an analog fire control computer, which created a firing solution. This was passed on to the gun turrets in the form of gun elevation and bearing, to allow an effective salvo to be fired. The process was then updated in preparation for the next salvo.

range from their airfields in Egypt. So, at 0900hrs on Sunday, the last group of fighters turned for home and the convoy was left without air cover at the most dangerous phase of the voyage. If the Italian fleet made contact, that would come in the afternoon. Until then, the real threat to the convoy came from the air. Despite the steadily deteriorating weather, visibility was still fairly good that morning, which increased the chances of the convoy being spotted and attacked by enemy bombers.

Sure enough, the first attack came just after 0930hrs. First, shadowing aircraft were detected, approaching from the south, which then circled the convoy at a safe distance. Relays of these shadowers – Italian Savoia-Marchetti S.79 bombers – would continue to circle the convoy throughout the day. Then, two groups of six S.79s appeared from the south, one flying at high level, the other approaching at sea level. By then, the convoy was ready for them, with a protective inner ring in place of Jellicoe's Hunt-class escort destroyers and an outer ring of destroyers from the 14th Destroyer Flotilla. The high-flying attackers were engaged by the AA cruisers, and they dropped their ordnance short of the convoy and then turned away towards Cyrenaica. As for the torpedo bombers, Capt. Nicholl described the attack as 'futile', as the 45cm (17.7in) Fiume torpedoes were all dropped at extreme range, almost 2 miles from the convoy, and so were easily avoided.

However, other air attacks followed, and would last throughout the day. The first attack set the pattern – small groups of aircraft making attacks, rather than one coordinated, concentrated attack. As the Convoy Commodore put it, 'During that afternoon and evening we had no less than 16 bombing attacks from the Luftwaffe and three torpedo bombing attacks. I had opened out the convoy so that each ship could safely take avoiding action independently. Whilst during the torpedo bombing attacks I manoeuvred the convoy as a whole to avoid the torpedoes – no ship was hit or even damaged by near misses.'

Italian and British fleet operations, 21–22 March

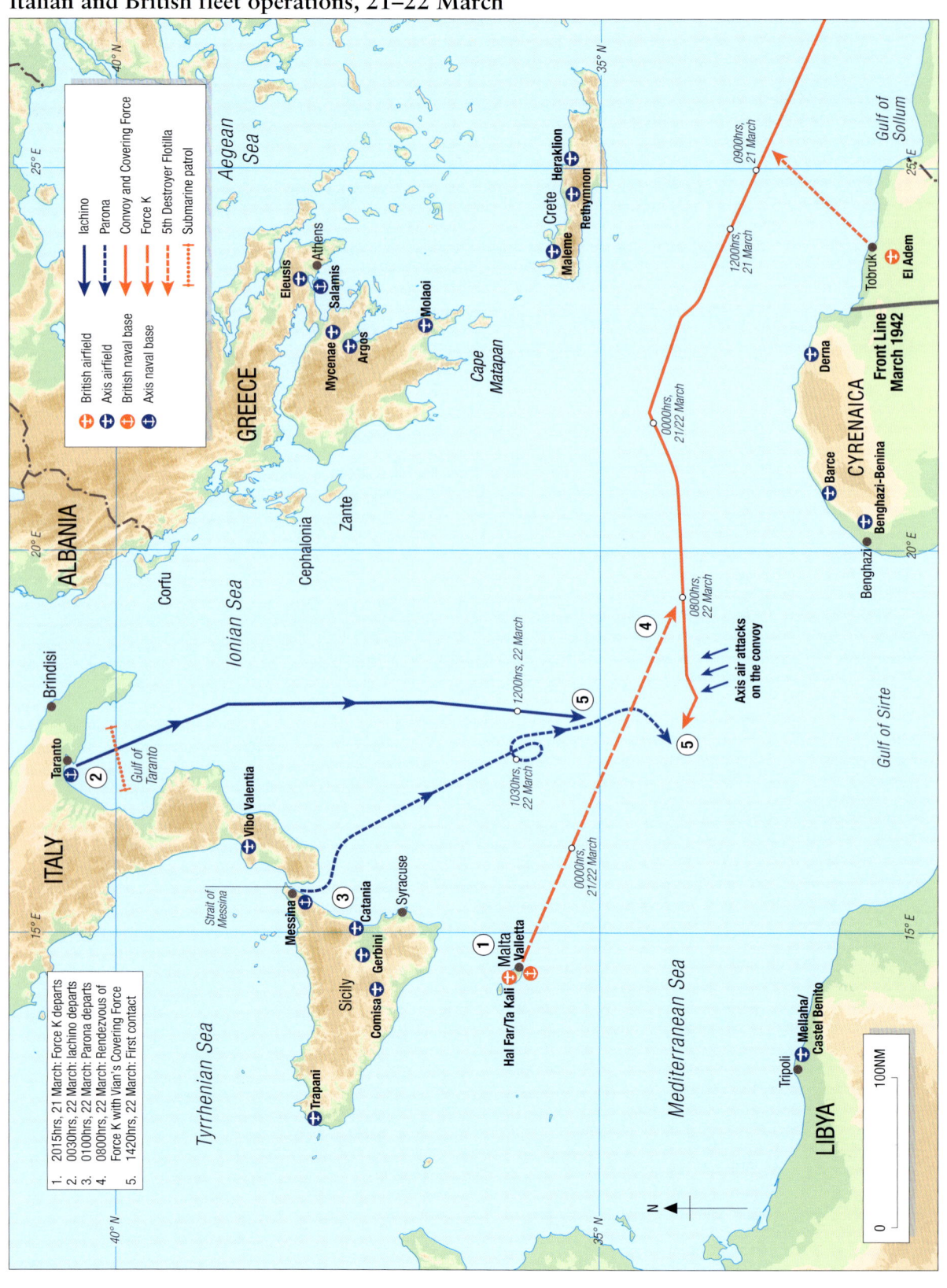

As the morning wore on though, the anticipated air attacks didn't come. This reflected the disorder in Cyrenaica following the diversionary bombing raids by the RAF. Only the Italian 131° Gruppo Aerosilurianti operating from Benghazi, 150 miles to the south-east, had managed to launch a morning attack, however unsuccessful it might have been. So, as the air warning radar screens remained clear of contacts, Vian relaxed slightly. Still, with noon approaching, the threat of encountering the Italian battlefleet was increasing. All of his captains – with the exception of the two from Force K – already had their standing orders, and knew what to do. Vian was confident that he and his men were ready for whatever might lie ahead.

'ENEMY DRIVEN OFF'

As the afternoon watch began (1200–1600hrs), Vian fully expected to make contact with an Italian surface force at some point over the next few hours. The precis of an Ultra report forwarded a few hours earlier by Cunningham and the sighting by the British submarine meant that the Italians were at sea, and they would be hunting for him. Convoy MW-10 and its escorts had endured air attacks all morning, but if the predominant threat was now from enemy surface warships rather than aircraft, then Vian needed to re-order the formation of the convoy's covering forces. In effect, this meant moving from an open anti-aircraft posture to one better suited to a surface action. When the order was given, the convoy alone would maintain its current formation.

That afternoon, the close escorts, Cdr Jellicoe's five remaining escort destroyers, had been deployed in a protective ring around the convoy to provide it with an AA defence. If facing a surface threat, these little warships would reform into a single line and take up a position a little to the north of the convoy – the direction the Italians were most likely to appear from. Similarly, Group 6, the two designated smoke layers (the light AA cruiser *Carlisle* and the escort destroyer *Avon Vale*), had also been kept close to the convoy to augment anti-aircraft defences. When ordered, these would move ahead of the convoy, ready to lay a smokescreen if the need arose.

The aged C-class light cruiser HMS *Carlisle* was launched in 1918, and two decades later was considered obsolete. However, in 1939 *Carlisle*, together with sister ships *Cairo* and *Calcutta*, was converted into an AA cruiser, and so given a new lease of life. At Second Sirte, under the command of Capt. Douglas Neame, *Carlisle* protected the convoy, together with the escort destroyer HMS *Avon Vale*, by making up a smoke screen detachment to hide it from Italian surface ships.

This redeployment was a pre-arranged manoeuvre, to be carried out when Vian gave the order. For the moment the air threat remained high, so Convoy MW-10 and its escorts maintained their current formation and continued on their current course, heading west-south-west (250°) at 12kts. That afternoon, Vian's other warships were to the west and north-west of the convoy, and so were more likely to contact the enemy before the convoy did. That, of course, assumed that the Italians were heading directly towards them from Taranto. In case they didn't, Vian had to be ready to redeploy his warships wherever they were needed to protect the convoy. That afternoon, Vian was sanguine that he and his men were as ready for the Italians as they could be.

The first sign of trouble came just before 1330hrs. An Italian IMAM Ro.43 floatplane appeared from the north-east and circled around behind Vian's cruisers and destroyers, before heading on towards the south. The floatplane was the type carried on board Italian battleships and the larger cruisers, which confirmed that the Italians were at sea, somewhere to the north of the British. The biplane quickly sighted the small convoy, but when Jellicoe's Close Escort opened fire the floatplane banked and climbed away, heading back out of range. Then it flew on to a spot 2 miles ahead of the convoy and then turned to the west–south-west, along the convoy's projected track. The floatplane's two-man crew began dropping flares along this route. The only reason for this was to help guide in another air formation or to help an Italian surface force locate the convoy and learn what course it was taking. It was an ominous sign.

Almost on cue, at 1348hrs, a formation of eight German bomb-armed Ju 88s appeared from the north. Unsurprisingly, they didn't head towards Vian's warships. Instead, they made for the convoy. The escort destroyers opened fire, and the ferocity of the barrage appeared to daunt the German pilots. They skirted around the convoy and formed up for the attack about 3 miles to the south of it. The Germans, all from II/KG 77, divided into two groups before making their approach, which was launched at 1418hrs. It lasted for around ten minutes. In the end, these attacks were half-hearted. Most of their 250kg bombs were released too early and no hits were scored, or even close misses recorded. By then, though, Vian had other problems to deal with.

At 1410hrs, lookouts in *Euryalus* spotted smoke on the northern horizon, on a compass bearing of 350° – slightly forward of the starboard beam. This could only be the Italian surface fleet. Sure enough, seven minutes later, at 1417hrs, Capt. Bush of *Euryalus* signalled Vian a mile ahead of him in *Cleopatra*, reporting that three ships could be seen, hull down to the north, some 14 miles away. Two minutes later, they were spotted by lookouts in the destroyer *Legion*, part of Capt. Nicholl's Force K, 2 miles to the south of the British AA cruisers. The enemy was in sight. So, at 1420hrs, Vian hoisted a signal, ordering the convoy and his Covering Force to move into close formation.

At the same time, Vian requested that the Convoy Commodore turn his ships away from the approaching enemy and to steer towards the south-west. On board *Breconshire*, Capt. Colin Hutchinson complied and prepared to turn his box formation of four merchantmen to port onto the new heading. At that moment though, Jellicoe's five close escorts were busy seeing off the enemy air attack. So Hutchinson delayed the course change until the last of the Ju 88s departed towards the north-west. Then, at 1430hrs,

For the most part, for anti-shipping operations the aircraft of Fliegerkorps X used 250kg SC 250 general-purpose bombs. A Ju 88 of the kind shown here carried a 'stick' of four of these bombs, mounted externally, as the bomber's two internal bomb bays proved less effective against maritime targets. A Ju 87 Stuka carried one of these bombs, mounted under the fuselage.

he gave the order. Slowly, the ponderous merchantmen turned onto their new heading of 220°. On that course, the swell that was now hitting their port beam made station-keeping tricky, but at least it took the convoy away from the approaching enemy ships. As they altered course, the convoy was accompanied by its smokescreen force, *Carlisle* and *Avon Vale*.

For his part, Cdr Jellicoe gathered his five escort destroyers, and formed them into a line abreast formation, stationed half a mile astern of the merchantmen – the point closest to the enemy. For the moment, the convoy was safe, at least from this new surface threat, as Vian's cruisers and destroyers now lay between MW-10 and the approaching Italians. Still, the lookouts in the escorts remained vigilant, peering towards the north, beyond Vian's cruisers, which was clearly visible a mile or more off their starboard quarter. For the moment, only Vian's force could see the enemy. At 1427hrs, Capt. Bush of *Euryalus* reported four more ships heading towards him, in line abreast, now just 12 miles away, on a compass bearing of 015°. That was almost directly off the cruiser's starboard beam.

Cdr Richard Jessel commanding the destroyer *Legion* also reported sighting a single ship approaching from the same direction, although it was unclear if this was one of the four or it was another sighting entirely. A minute or so earlier, at 1426hrs, the Italian lookouts spotted the British cruisers and destroyers to the south. When Bush's report reached him on the bridge of *Cleopatra*, Vian thought it was probably Adm. Iachino's flagship *Littorio* approaching with an escorting screen of destroyers. This was the worst possible news, as Vian had nothing that could match the Italian battleship's firepower. Instead, he would have to counter *Littorio* using smokescreens and manoeuvring. He had to keep the Italian battleship away from the convoy at all costs.

In fact, what the lookouts on board *Euryalus* had seen wasn't *Littorio* and accompanying destroyers. It was V. Adm. Parona's three cruisers and

First contact with the enemy, 1415–1530hrs, 22 March 1942

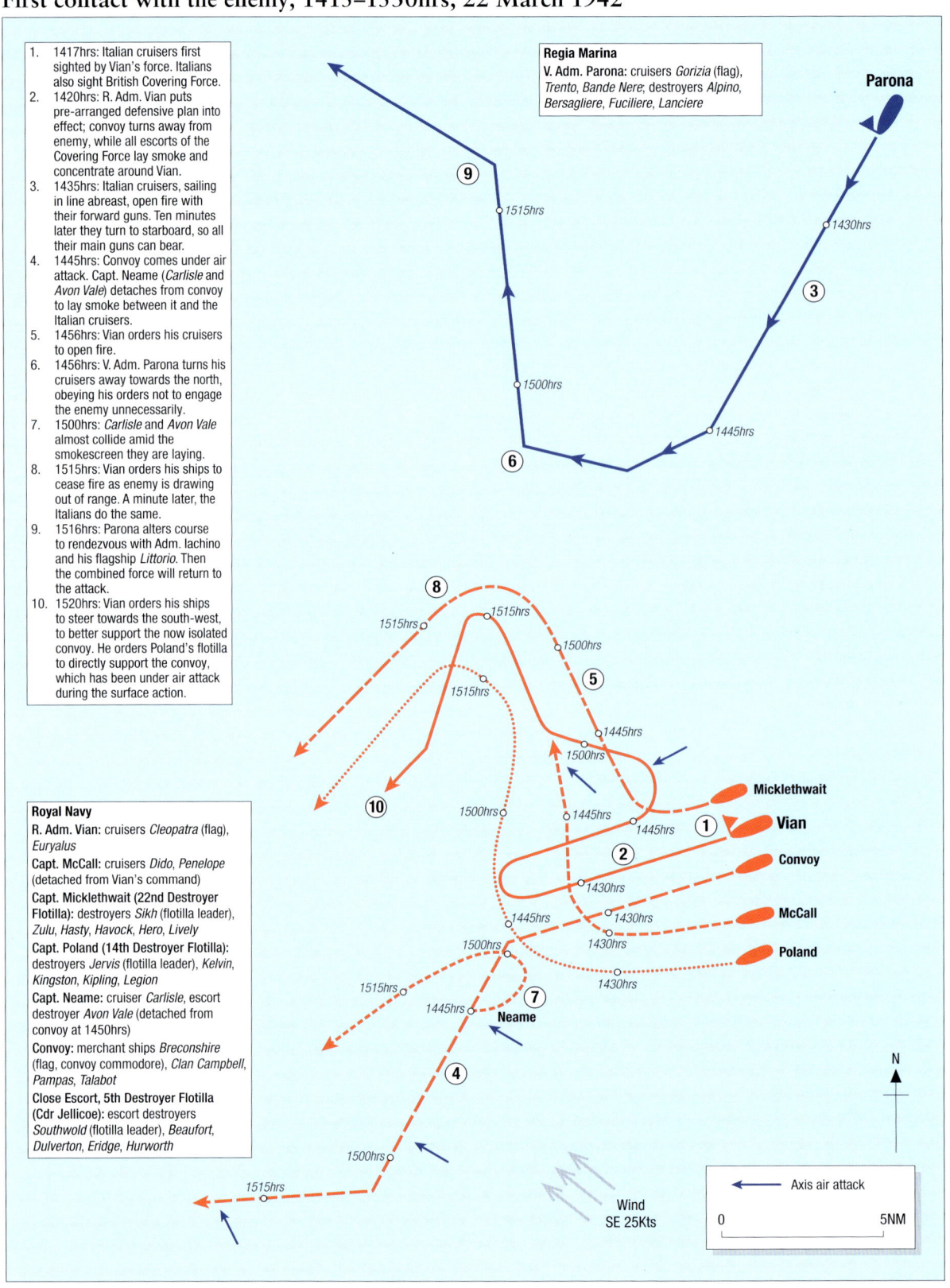

The Italian heavy cruiser *Gorizia*, pictured in Taranto harbour. During the battle this powerful cruiser was the flagship of V. Adm. Parona. *Gorizia* was the last surviving member of the Zara class – the three others had all been sunk the previous spring, in the Battle of Matapan.

their own destroyer screen approaching from the north-east with the cruisers deployed in line abreast, with his flagship *Gorizia* flanked by *Trento* and *Banda Nere* to port. Each cruiser was 3,000yds from each other. The four escorting destroyers (*Alpino*, *Bersagliere*, *Fuciliere* and *Lanciere*) were in line ahead, 2 miles off the starboard beam of *Gorizia*. Iachino's battleship was still some 6 miles to the north-east of Parona, heading west, accompanied by three destroyers (*Ascari*, *Aviere* and *Alfredo Oriani*). The Italian cruisers had been labouring in the rough seas, with the south-easterly wind hitting them on their port quarter and whipping up the seas. As a result, for the sake of his destroyers, Parona had reduced his force's speed to 22kts. So too had Iachino, his battleship still out of sight of the cruisers. Both groups had been at action stations since 1340hrs, after the report from *Trento*'s seaplane had been radioed in.

Vian's signal to his Covering Force at 1420hrs was 'carry out pre-arranged plan'. Essentially, this meant forming up into a closer formation. At that moment, his cruisers and destroyers were scattered over several miles of sea. *Cleopatra*, with *Euryalus* astern, was heading west-south-west, making 12kts. *Dido* was 3 miles off the flagship's port beam, steaming ahead of the four-ship convoy, which was 2 miles astern of the cruiser. The convoy was still accompanied by *Carlisle*, *Avon Vale* and Jellicoe's five escort destroyers. The destroyers *Sikh*, *Lively*, *Hero* and *Havock* of Capt. Micklethwait's 22nd Flotilla were screening Vian's cruisers, steaming ahead of Vian's flagship, while two more, *Zulu* and *Hasty*, were accompanying *Cleopatra* and *Euryalus*. Five miles to the south of Vian, ranging ahead of the convoy were Capt. Albert Poland's 14th Flotilla destroyers *Jervis*, *Kelvin*, *Kingston* and *Kipling*. At that moment, this made Vian's two cruisers and two accompanying destroyers the closest British warships to the enemy.

Vian's pre-arranged plan was laid down in standing orders issued before the operation began. The aim was to bring his force together, so he was better able to command it during a surface action. So, on receiving the signal, Poland's destroyers of the 14th Flotilla, which were already in line ahead,

The AA cruiser HMS *Dido*, namesake of the class. During the battle *Dido*, commanded by Capt. Henry McCall, was paired with Capt. Angus Nicholl's HMS *Penelope*, the last remaining light cruiser of Force K, the veteran Malta Strike Force. They followed 2 miles astern of *Cleopatra* and *Euryalus*, acting as Vian's reserve.

altered course to the north-west, to place themselves ahead of Vian. Similarly, Micklethwait's 22nd Flotilla also turned to the north-west, although it remained in its two divisions, with *Zulu* and *Hasty* forming their own small division. However, due to a clerical oversight, one part of Vian's command hadn't received these standing orders. Force K, commanded by Capt. Nicholl of the light cruiser *Penelope*, had only been attached to Vian's command the day before while in Malta. So, as the other ships raced to take up their new stations, *Penelope* and the destroyer *Legion* were taken by surprise. Fortunately for Vian, Nicholl was an enterprising officer, and he reacted well.

As Nicholl put it later:

The convoy and all of the ships of the escort then began moving in various directions at high speed. I, unfortunately, had no knowledge of any pre-arranged plan – no previous orders of any kind had reached *Penelope*. However, there is a well-tried course of action I had learned in my time in the destroyers: 'When in doubt, follow father!' So I tacked on to Vian's cruisers, and *Legion* joined the nearest destroyer division. Though I had no instructions, I had no difficulty in sensing what Vian wanted the cruisers to do.

To the south, Capt. Henry McCall of *Dido* also heeded the call, and turned north towards Vian. That meant that both of Vian's detached cruisers – *Dido* and *Penelope* – were heading at speed towards *Cleopatra* and *Euryalus*. This gave Vian the force he needed to counter the approaching Italians, which by now had been tentatively identified as three heavy cruisers. Afterwards, McCall wrote, 'Vian led us towards the enemy at high speed, and all the cruisers made smoke.' In other words, Vian's immediate response, after the enemy ships were identified at 1417hrs, was to turn towards them. He didn't even wait for McCall and Nicholl to catch up. Instead, he ordered his flag captain, Guy Grantham, to turn *Cleopatra* round to the north, and he headed straight for the centre of the Italian line. In *Euryalus*, Capt. Bush gave the order to follow the flagship. As *Cleopatra* began laying a black oily smokescreen from its funnels, Bush followed suit.

Meanwhile, at 1429hrs, on board *Gorizia*, three minutes after first sighting Vian's cruisers, Parona gave the order to turn his force to starboard, and to head north, directly away from the enemy. This was in line with his orders, to make contact with the enemy and then 'to communicate news without engaging'. This had the added advantage of closing the range with Iachino in *Littorio*, and possibly even drawing the British warships away from the convoy and closer to the Italian battleship. Parona had strict written orders, specifying exactly what he had to do. This didn't include bringing on a general engagement. Meanwhile, Vian's priority was to screen the convoy. So, at 1433hrs, he turned *Cleopatra* and *Euryalus* towards the north-east to extend the smokescreen while still reducing the range.

Taken from the bridge of *Euryalus*, this shows the effectiveness of the smokescreen laid by *Cleopatra* ahead of *Euryalus* while both ships engaged the Italian battlefleet some 8 miles away.

As a result, Vian's two cruisers were racing north-eastwards at 32kts, in line ahead, while 2 miles behind them, *Dido* and *Penelope* were converging with each other from different locations. At the same time, both cruisers were heading in the general direction of Vian's flagship, which was now to the north of them. Essentially then, the British cruisers had formed into two divisions, each of two ships. Their turn towards the enemy was spotted by the Italians, who were already turning away from the British. At 1435hrs, Parona's three cruisers opened fire with their after turrets, at the extreme range of 21,000m – the equivalent of 10½ miles.[1] At that range, it was wildly optimistic to expect a hit.

This turn away didn't suit Parona, who wanted to continue the fight, regardless of his orders. He argued later that, as he was out of range of his opponents, he wasn't really engaging fully with the enemy in a gunnery duel. Technically, he wasn't going against Iachino's orders. So, the Italian commander ordered his ships to continue their turn to starboard until they had completed a full circle. By 1436hrs, they had resumed their original course, towards the south-west. To continue on, though, would bring his ships closer to the British cruisers than he intended, which were then steering to the east-north-east. Four minutes later, when Vian altered slightly more to the north-east, Parona decided to turn away to prevent the range from decreasing further. For him, it was all a matter of gunnery and ballistics.

The 8in (20.3cm) guns of his heavy cruisers had a range of up to 28,000m (15 miles), and even his light cruiser's 6in (15.2cm) guns had a maximum range of 12 miles. This was much better than the reported 13,000yd (6½ mile) effective range of Vian's AA cruisers. In other words, while Parona could hit Vian, the British commander couldn't hit back. At 1445hrs, with Vian continuing on to the north-east, Parona ordered a turn to starboard

---

1 In naval gunnery, ranges were generally measured in sea miles of 2,000yds, rather than in nautical miles (which are 2,025yds or 1,852m).

FIRST CLASH BETWEEN THE CRUISER SQUADRONS, 1456HRS, 22 MARCH 1942 (PP.48–49)

At 1436hrs, after the approaching Italian warships were spotted to the north, R. Adm. Philip Vian gave orders for his ships to lay a smokescreen using funnel smoke. While the convoy and its Close Escort were shepherded away, Vian closed the range with the approaching Italians. Less than ten minutes later R. Adm. Angelo Parana ordered his 3rd Cruiser Division (**1**) to turn to the west, so all his ships' guns could bear. His flagship, the Zara-class heavy cruiser *Gorizia* (**2**) was in the lead, followed by the heavy cruiser *Trento* (**3**), namesake of the class. Bringing up the rear of the line was the Condottiere-class (first group) light cruiser *Giovanni delle Bande Nere* (**4**) armed with 6in guns. At 1655hrs Vian turned onto a parallel course, and a minute later his flagship *Cleopatra* and sister ship *Euryalus* opened fire, at a range of 10 miles. These Dido-class AA cruisers were armed with 5.25in guns, which lacked the firepower of their Italian opponents, as well as the range. The first British salvos fell short (**5**), but so too did the Italian 8in and 6in salvos (**6**). Accuracy was hindered by the increasingly rough seas (**7**) and strong wind. This wind cloaked the British convoy Vian was protecting from Parona and so, when the British opened fire, proving they had the range to damage his force, Parona broke off the action and turned away to the north. His orders were to try and lure Vian after him, onto the guns of the battleship *Littorio*. Vian, though, decided to protect the convoy, and so the action ended after less than 20 minutes of firing. Neither side managed to score a hit on the other.

The Italian heavy cruiser *Gorizia* in action during the battle. *Gorizia*, the flagship of V. Adm. Parona's 3rd Cruiser Division, was engaged in two clashes with Vian's Covering Force, firing 226 8in (20.3cm) shells during the battle. This photograph was taken from the heavy cruiser *Trento*, on a parallel course off its port beam.

onto a west-south-westerly course of 235°. This effectively put the two forces on nearly parallel courses, a little less than 12 miles apart. At the same time, the Italians moved into a line formation, with the flagship *Gorizia* in the lead, followed by *Trento* and then *Banda Nere*. This meant that all the main guns on the Italian cruisers could now bear on the enemy.

As soon as the Italian ships steadied on their new course, they resumed firing at the British cruisers. However, the smokescreen laid so promptly by Vian's cruisers was a problem, making spotting difficult. By this stage, it wasn't just the British cruisers that were making smoke. All of Micklethwait and Poland's destroyers were doing the same. Of these, Micklethwait's screen was more effective, as his destroyers were now ranged on either side of Vian's cruisers, with his own *Sikh* accompanied by *Lively*, *Hero* and *Havock* ahead of the flagship, and *Zulu* and *Hasty* following behind *Euryalus*. The oily black funnel smoke they created, together with the white chemical smoke from dischargers at their sterns, produced a wall of smoke some 3 miles long. With the smoke drifting towards the Italian ships, this created a murky almost impenetrable barrier.

At 1450hrs, Parona ordered another change to 280°, to open the range slightly. Vian took time to react, as his cruisers were under air attack at the time. Still, by 1455hrs, the German bombers were flying off, having completed their attack, and Vian duly turned *Cleopatra* and *Euryalus* onto a parallel course to the Italian line, which was now a little over 10 miles or 18,000yds to the north. A minute later, at 1456hrs, Vian gave the order to open fire. The effectiveness of the British 5.25in guns came as an unpleasant surprise to Parona. Although the initial British salvos fell a mile short of the Italian ships, their reach far exceeded what the Italians had expected.

Intelligence reports had suggested that these British quick-firing guns had a maximum range of 19,000yds, and an effective one of 13,000. In fact, their maximum range was 24,000yds. With a rate of fire of around 8rpm, the British fire control teams in *Cleopatra* and *Euryalus* quickly corrected the range, and the shell salvos crept closer to the Italian cruisers. While the chances of the British scoring a hit at that range were slight, their ability to reach the Italians at all came as a shock to Parona. His orders were explicit – not to engage the enemy. So, the Italian commander was left with no option but to turn away. At 1456hrs, Parona ordered his ships to immediately turn away towards the north. This meant that they returned to their old line abreast formation, with the cruisers well spaced out, around 2 miles apart from each other.

During the battle the destroyers HMS *Zulu* and HMS *Hasty*, a detachment of Capt. Micklethwait's 22nd Destroyer Flotilla, were ordered to provide a smokescreen to protect Vian's cruisers. This picture, taken from *Dido*, shows them laying a thick screen of black funnel smoke.

For the moment, the gun duel continued as the Italian cruisers still fired their after guns at the British, who responded with full broadsides of their lighter guns, at maximum elevation. At around 1501hrs, a salvo of 6in shells fired by *Bande Nere* successfully straddled both *Cleopatra* and *Euryalus*. The shells from the two Italian heavy cruisers continued to fall short, their rangefinder teams undoubtedly struggling to gauge the range accurately due to the smoke. For his part, Vian had *Cleopatra* and *Euryalus* dodge in and out of the smokescreen every few minutes to throw off the Italians' fire. However, it didn't really help the British fire control teams, and their 5.25in salvos, fired at extreme range, failed to achieve a straddle, let alone a hit.

At 1508hrs, Vian ordered *Cleopatra* to turn hard to port towards the north, to pursue the Italians. *Euryalus* duly followed, and the two wings of destroyers turned too, to conform to this new course. The result was that Vian was keeping pace with the Italians as both groups of ships sped north. Vian was delighted as this meant the enemy was heading away from the convoy, but he was wary too, thanks to the reports that an Italian battleship was at sea and presumably was intending to attack the convoy. By 1510hrs, when *Dido* and *Penelope* coming up astern of Vian were subjected to another German air attack, Vian checked the plot, and saw that he was almost 18 miles to the north of the convoy. With all four British cruisers haring after the Italian cruisers, MW-10 was left dangerously exposed.

At that moment, the Italian cruisers were heading north at 25kts, in line abreast, some 11 miles ahead of the British flagship. *Euryalus* was off *Cleopatra*'s port quarter, so the cruiser's forward guns were not blocked by the flagship. Vian's two lead cruisers were accompanied by Micklethwait's 22nd Destroyer Flotilla, with four destroyers led by *Sikh* off *Cleopatra*'s port beam, and two more, led by *Zulu*, off the starboard beam of *Euryalus*. Astern of Vian, *Dido* and *Penelope* were 2 miles away, with Capt. Poland's four destroyers of the 14th Flotilla also approaching the flagship, 2 miles astern of *Cleopatra* and 2 miles off the port beam of *Dido*. They were accompanied by the destroyer *Legion* from Force K, which had been detached by Capt. Nicholl of *Penelope*. This meant the whole of Vian's Covering Force – four cruisers and 11 destroyers – was pursuing the Italians, and moving steadily away from the convoy they were supposed to protect.

Far ahead of Vian, on board *Gorizia*, Parona was checking his plot too, and could see that if Vian continued to chase him, he would be led directly onto the 15in (38.1cm) guns of the battleship *Littorio*. So, he was content to keep drawing Vian after his three cruisers. While they sped north, the

This is one of a sequence of photographs taken from the open bridge of HMS *Euryalus* during the battle. This shows HMS *Cleopatra* weaving across the cruiser's bows, just a few hundred yards away, using its funnels to lay a thick black smokescreen.

four destroyers attached to Parona's command were keeping station with the cruisers, some 4 miles off the port beam of *Trento*. However, Parona had lost sight of the convoy, which was completely hidden behind the smokescreens laid by Vian's Covering Force and by *Carlisle* and *Avon Vale*. That really didn't matter though, as once Vian's cruisers were dealt with, the Italians could turn south again and destroy the convoy. According to radio chatter, it was already under heavy air attack. That meant that the Italian battlefleet might be spared the trouble of hunting down Convoy MW-10.

Meanwhile, far to the south, the convoy was dealing with that air attack. The first of these had come at 1445hrs, soon after Parona's Italian force had been spotted to the north. The high-altitude attack on the convoy by 12 Ju 88s didn't achieve any hits, thanks largely to the heavy fire put up by the escort destroyers. Eight minutes later, though, at 1453hrs, nine Ju 88s spotted *Cleopatra* and *Euryalus*, and moved in for the attack, approaching from the east. This was a pop-up toss bombing attack, where the twin-engine bombers approached just above sea level, then climbed at the last moment before releasing their bombs. These were then thrown upwards and forwards, before curving towards the target. In this instance, the attempt failed, largely due to the combined fire of the two British cruisers, which caused most of the attackers to release too early. Still, this attack was particularly distracting for Vian, as until then the gunnery teams of the cruisers had been preparing to engage the Italian cruisers.

But these were only the start of the relentless air attacks, which continued throughout the afternoon. At 1456hrs, another group of six Ju 88s attacked the convoy from high altitude, while less than five minutes later, four more approaching at low level launched another toss-bombing attack against *Dido*. Both attacks proved unsuccessful. What really helped the British were the smokescreens that were now enveloping just about every warship, as well as the convoy. This created its own problems, though, as a little after 1500hrs, *Carlisle* and *Avon Vale* almost collided amid the smoke. When it happened, they'd been turning to make another

A German Junkers Ju 88A twin-engined medium bomber. These aircraft of Fliegerkorps X posed the greatest threat to the convoy as it passed through Bomb Alley on its way to Malta. However, when these aircraft finally attacked the convoy on 22 March, their assaults were in small *Schwärme* ('Swarms', singular *Schwärm*) of four to eight aircraft, which were driven off by the fire of the convoy's Close Escort.

smoke-laying run 2 miles to the north-east of the convoy. The warships scraped down each other's hulls, damaging paintwork but nothing else. By then, the gunnery duel between the two groups of cruisers was drawing to a close. At 1515hrs, Vian ordered his cruisers to cease fire. Almost by mutual agreement, a minute later the Italians did the same.

Vian ordered a somewhat wishful signal to be sent off to Adm. Cunningham in Alexandria, which read 'Enemy Driven Off'. This, though, was somewhat premature. V. Adm. Parona was merely following orders, declining an engagement and attempting to draw the British Covering Force towards Iachino. Meanwhile, the Italian battleship and escorts had altered course at 1353hrs and were now heading south on a course of 200°. The aim was to rendezvous with Parona, and then the two groups could launch a joint attack that would almost certainly be able to deal with both Vian and the convoy. As for the British, at 1515hrs, Vian also ordered *Cleopatra* and *Euryalus* to break off contact with the enemy. After a neat turn away to the south, the cruisers settled on a new course 15 minutes later. They were now heading towards the south-west, away from the enemy and closer to the convoy.

Dido and *Penelope* did the same, taking up station 2 miles off the port quarter of the flagship. All of the British cruisers were now in line astern formation, with *Euryalus* following *Cleopatra* and *Penelope* astern of *Dido*. Capt. Poland's destroyer flotilla kept station off the flagship's port beam,

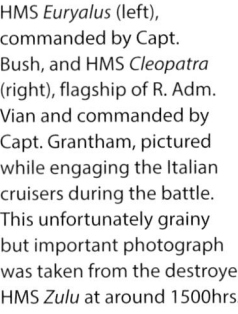

HMS *Euryalus* (left), commanded by Capt. Bush, and HMS *Cleopatra* (right), flagship of R. Adm. Vian and commanded by Capt. Grantham, pictured while engaging the Italian cruisers during the battle. This unfortunately grainy but important photograph was taken from the destroyer HMS *Zulu* at around 1500hrs.

while Capt. Micklethwait's one did the same, 4 miles to the north. On that course, Vian expected to regain visual contact with the convoy at around 1600hrs, which by that stage was heading due west. As for the Italians, all visual and radar contact had been lost. Vian sincerely hoped it would stay that way.

SECOND CONTACT

By 1520hrs, V. Adm. Parona's force had lost contact with the British. However, lookouts had seen Vian's force turn away to the south-west, which meant the enemy was no longer heading towards *Littorio*. Still, Parona was sanguine that he would affect a rendezvous with Iachino within the next hour, and that together the two Italian groups could intercept both Vian's Covering Force and the convoy. After withdrawing to the north, Parona continued on, despite the buffeting his ships were getting from the rough seas, and the strong wind from the south-east, which brought mist, spray and poor visibility in its wake. Still, there were sections of better visibility among the mist patches, and it was in one of these, a little after 1600hrs, that lookouts in the destroyer *Bersagliere* spotted the *Littorio*.

Despite his rank, Ammiraglio desginato d'Armata (Acting Admiral) Angelo Iachino was arguably the most experienced senior commander in the Italian navy by 1942. Known popularly as 'Jachino', he was an intelligent and skilled strategist and after the war wrote extensively on Italian naval matters.

The battleship was 8 miles away to the west, heading towards the south-south-east, with the three destroyers in line ahead half a mile off its port beam. Once the sighting report was passed to Parona in *Gorizia*, he turned his force around to port, and still in a line abreast formation he set off on a converging course towards the south-east. At 1618hrs, the two Italian forces rendezvoused, and Parona's force was ordered to take up station 3 miles off the battleship's starboard beam. His destroyers remained in line ahead, 2 miles further to the west of *Gorizia*. This meant that with the battleship's three destroyers still off *Littorio*'s port beam, the whole Italian battlefleet was spread out over some 9 miles of sea. It had also turned onto a south-westerly course. Iachino was confident that he would encounter the British and their slow-moving convoy within the next 30 minutes. He was quite right. The second clash of the battle was about to begin.

Since the first phase of the battle had ended, the convoy had been under regular air attack from small groups of Axis aircraft. At 1510hrs, the convoy had turned west, steering 270°. It was now protected by four escort destroyers, with *Dulverton* and *Eridge* off its port beam and *Southwold* and *Beaufort* to starboard. The AA cruiser *Carlisle* and the escort destroyer *Avon Vale* were 7 miles away to the north, but once contact was broken with the Italian cruisers they headed at speed towards the south-west to rejoin the convoy. Once this rendezvous was achieved at 1550hrs, the already potent firepower of the convoy was given a significant boost.

EVENTS

1. 1637–1640hrs: Italian warships approaching from the north are sighted by both *Sikh* and *Euryalus*.

2. 1641hrs: Vian orders 22nd Destroyer Flotilla to make smokescreen and cover force and convoy. 14th Destroyer Flotilla ordered to close with convoy, while convoy and its Close Escort ordered to turn away towards the south-west.

3. 1643hrs: Vian turns to port and opens fire with *Cleopatra* and *Euryalus*. Moments later, *Littorio* and the three Italian cruisers return fire with their forward guns.

4. 1645hrs: A 6in salvo fired by *Bande Nere* straddles *Cleopatra* and the British cruiser is hit.

5. 1647hrs: V. Adm. Parona turns his cruisers to starboard to allow all of his ships' main guns to fire.

6. 1648hrs: *Euryalus* receives minor damage from a near miss, but moments later Vian's cruisers are hidden from the enemy by the smokescreen laid by the 22nd Destroyer Flotilla.

7. 1655hrs: Unable to see the enemy, Vian turns his cruisers to the east to see if the Italians are attempting to approach the convoy from the east.

8. 1711hrs: Having emerged from the smokescreen, Vian can see there are no Italian ships to the north-east attempting to circle around behind the British. So, he orders his cruisers to turn to the west to regain contact with the enemy. His cruisers are also subjected to an air attack (1710hrs).

9. 1720hrs: Having attempted to work around the smokescreen to the south-west, when a gap appears in it, Iachino has a clear view of the 22nd Destroyer Flotilla's destroyers. *Littorio* opens fire at them.

10. 1720hrs: Destroyer *Havock* hit and disabled by a shell fired from *Littorio*.

11. 1721hrs: Capt. Micklethwait, commanding the 22nd Destroyer Flotilla, lays more smoke to cloak *Havock* and circles to starboard to launch a torpedo spread at *Littorio*. However, as the range is really too great, Micklethwait abandons the attempt and retires behind the smokescreen again.

12. 1732hrs: *Euryalus* sights Italians to north-west. Vian orders his cruisers to alter course to the west to close the range and engage the enemy and also provide support for 22nd Destroyer Flotilla.

13. 1744hrs: *Littorio* and the three Italian cruisers have a clear view of the British 22nd Destroyer Flotilla through the smoke and fire successive salvos at them.

14. 1748hrs: Although no direct hits are made, *Sikh* and *Lively* are slightly damaged and Micklethwait withdraws into the smokescreen after *Sikh* launches two torpedoes at the Italian battleship.

15. 1750hrs: With no clear enemy targets in sight, Iachino orders his force to turn towards the south to locate and destroy the convoy.

THE MAIN ENCOUNTER, 1640–1750HRS, 22 MARCH 1942

Although the first contact between the British and the approaching Italian battlefleet took place in the early afternoon, it was a fleeting one, as the Italian cruisers withdrew as they had been ordered to do. However, after a rendezvous with Adm. Iachino's flagship, the modern battleship *Littorio*, the combined Italian force returned to renew contact and to seek out and destroy the British convoy. What followed was a running battle as R. Adm. Vian's heavily outgunned force sparred with the Italians, while laying smokescreens to protect themselves and to screen the vital convoy a few miles away to the south. Vian's objective was to protect the convoy at all costs in the face of a determined and powerful opponent.

ITALIAN REGIA MARINA
A. Adm. Iachino's force: battleship *Littorio* (flagship) and attached destroyers *Ascari*, *Aviere* and *Alfredo Oriani*
B. V. Adm. Parona's force (3rd Cruiser Division): heavy cruisers *Gorizia* (flagship) and *Trento*, light cruiser *Giovanni delle Bande Nere*, accompanied by 13th Destroyer Flotilla: destroyers *Alpino*, *Bersagliere*, *Fuciliere* and *Lanciere*

BRITISH ROYAL NAVY
1. Convoy MW-10 and Close Escort:
   Close Escort (Capt. Neame): light AA cruiser *Carlisle* (flag)
   5th Destroyer Flotilla (Cdr Jellicoe): escort destroyers *Southwold* (flotilla leader), *Avon Vale*, *Beaufort*, *Dulverton* and *Eridge*
2. R. Adm. Vian's Covering Force (Force B): AA cruisers *Cleopatra* (flag), *Dido* and *Euryalus*, light cruiser *Penelope*, with 22nd Destroyer Flotilla destroyers *Zulu* and *Hasty* attached
3. 22nd Destroyer Flotilla (Capt. Micklethwait): destroyers *Sikh* (flotilla leader), *Havock*, *Hero* and *Lively*
4. 14th Destroyer Flotilla (Capt. Poland): destroyers *Jervis* (flotilla leader), *Kelvin*, *Kingston*, *Kipling* and *Legion*

The Dido-class AA cruiser HMS *Euryalus*, pictured in November 1941. The cruiser was passing northwards through the Suez Canal on its way to Alexandria by way of Port Said. The high threat of air attacks in the Mediterranean led to the British Admiralty forming a whole squadron of them for service with the Mediterranean Fleet.

Once they rejoined the convoy, *Carlisle* took up station ahead of it and *Avon Vale* was stationed immediately astern of it. Given the relatively small scale of the air attacks that afternoon, this was a powerful enough Close Escort for the convoy.

It certainly needed one. At 1524hrs, the air attacks resumed. The first was from Italian SM.79 Sparviero twin-engined bombers, which attacked from high altitude without scoring any hits. Eleven minutes later at 1535hrs, it was the turn of two more Sparvieros, this time attempting a torpedo attack at long range. The two 17.72in (45cm) torpedoes were easily sidestepped by the convoy, and passed harmlessly astern of it. At 1551hrs, just as *Carlisle* and *Avon Vale* were taking up position, it was the turn of six Ju 87 Stukas, but, again, a wall of close-range anti-aircraft fire forced the dive-bomber pilots to drop their ordnance early, and they flew off without even coming close to hitting one of their British targets.

More air attacks followed at 1609hrs and again at 1614hrs, the first by three Ju 87s, the second by six Ju 88s. The first was another dive-bomb attack, while the Ju 88s carried out a toss-bombing run. Neither achieved anything. In every case, the escorts were ready for them, helped greatly by the return of *Carlisle* with its Type 280 combined air search and anti-aircraft fire control radar. This meant the British could detect the attackers early, and be ready for them with a flak wall of 4in shells. The trouble was, with all of these small penny-packet attacks, the British escorts were forced to expend ammunition. By 1630hrs, when tallies were completed, *Carlisle* was down to 65 per cent of its original stock of 4in shells, but the Hunt-class escort destroyers were down to just 40 per cent. This was serious, as the convoy was still 150 miles from Malta.

When this report was passed to Vian at 1635hrs, he ordered Capt. Poland's 14th Destroyer Flotilla to detach itself from the Covering Force and to head south to reinforce the convoy's Close Escort. At that point, Vian felt that the air threat to the convoy was greater than any surface threat posed by the Italian Supermarina. In a few minutes, he would be proved very wrong. By 1640hrs, the British were as scattered as they had been two hours before, at the start of the first engagement. Both the convoy and its Close Escort was heading west, while 6 miles to the north, Vian was doing the same, with his cruisers in two columns, with *Dido* and *Penelope* a mile off the port beam of *Cleopatra* and *Euryalus*. Although they had been closing with the convoy, and were within sight of it, Vian decided to remain well to the north of it so he could intercept the enemy if it appeared from the north.

So, from 1610hrs, when Vian made that decision, his cruisers had been heading on a parallel course to the convoy. Just over a mile to the north of the flagship were Capt. Micklethwait's six destroyers, in line, with *Sikh* in the lead. Between Vian and the convoy, Capt. Poland's five destroyers had been in a similar position to the south of *Dido* and *Penelope*, but they were now heading towards the south-west, to reinforce the convoy's Close Escort. A little to the south of them, *Carlisle* and *Avon Vale* were between Poland and the convoy, laying yet more smoke. It was at this point, at 1637hrs, that a lookout on board the destroyer *Sikh* spotted the Italian battlefleet. It was about 10 miles away, heading towards the south-west at high speed.

For the second time that afternoon, the enemy was in sight. Directly north of *Zulu* were V. Adm. Parona's three cruisers and four destroyers. Moments later, lookouts also spotted a battleship, a little further away to the north-east, screened by three destroyers. The sighting report was flashed to Vian, who immediately ordered all his ships to make smoke. Three minutes later, at 1640hrs, the same enemy ships were spotted by *Euryalus*. Vian ordered his ships to edge towards the north slightly, while still making smoke. The exception was Poland's flotilla, which continued to head towards the convoy. The odds were not good – four cruisers and six destroyers against three cruisers, seven destroyers and a powerful modern battleship.

Vian, though, had correctly appraised the tactical situation. Iachino would be reluctant to send his largest ships into the smokescreen, where they could be ambushed by other hidden ships, or subjected to a sudden torpedo attack. For the British then, everything depended on laying down an effective smokescreen. First, at 1643hrs, Vian gave the order to open fire on the Italian cruisers. For *Cleopatra* and *Euryalus*, 10 miles was their maximum range, and so the chances of scoring a hit were low. Still, it showed aggression, and a willingness to fight regardless of the odds. This gesture, though, came at a price. Parona's cruisers immediately opened fire themselves, and at 1645hrs, a 6in shell, most probably from *Bande Nere*, struck *Cleopatra* amidships. The shell knocked out the flagship's radio communications and the Type 279 air search radar. It also killed 16 crew and wounded several others.

Afterwards, Iachino claimed Vian's flagship was hit by a 6in (15.2cm) shell fired by *Littorio*'s port side secondary battery, which was also engaging the British cruisers at the time. This is unlikely though, as at the time the battleship's main 15in (38.1cm) battery was targeting *Euryalus*, half a mile astern of Vian's flagship. In any case, this was impressive gunnery. If the shell came from *Bande Nere*, it was the Italian light cruiser's second salvo. It was also fired in increasingly rough seas at long range. As a result of that single 6in shell hit, Vian was reduced to issuing orders using signal lamps and flags, with *Euryalus* then passing on any orders by radio. It also

R. ADM. VIAN'S FLAGSHIP *CLEOPATRA* IS HIT, 1644HRS, 22 MARCH 1942 (PP.60–61)

Since the first clash ended at 1515hrs, R. Adm. Vian tried to gather his scattered Covering Force, but continued to lay smoke to protect the convoy several miles to the south. As the convoy was under air attack for much of the afternoon, Vian thinned his own force by sending half of his destroyers to reinforce the convoy's Close Escort. However, at 1640hrs the Italian cruisers reappeared to the north, although this time they were accompanied by Adm. Iachino's flagship, the battleship *Littorio*. Capt. Micklethwait's destroyers were to the north-east of *Cleopatra* (**1**), busily laying a thick smokescreen of funnel smoke (**2**). So too were the destroyers *Zulu* and *Hasty*, two miles to the north-west. While the smoked partially blocked the line of sight of the Italian heavy cruisers (**3**), the light cruiser *Giovanni delle Bande Nere* opened fire at 1643hrs (**4**). The range was just over 8 miles. *Cleopatra* and sister ship *Euryalus* duly returned fire (**5**). A minute later, though, *Cleopatra* was hit (**6**) by a 6in shell from *Bande Nere*. It was the Italian cruiser's second salvo. It struck the starboard front corner of the open bridge, killing or wounding several men, and knocking out the cruiser's radio and the fire control radar, which was mounted a little behind the point of impact (**7**). Moments later the Italian battleship *Littorio* appeared in sight to the north (**8**) and opened fire on *Euryalus*. That prompted Vian to withdraw his cruisers to port, into the cover of the smoke.

The Italian light cruiser *Giovanni delle Bande Nere* in action against Vian's cruisers in the late afternoon of 22 March. During the engagement a 6in (15.2cm) shell from *Bande Nere* struck Vian's flagship *Cleopatra*. In all the Italian cruiser fired 112 shells that afternoon.

revealed that the standard Italian gunnery, which had been relatively poor in other engagements, was now greatly improved, despite the challenging sea conditions and the smokescreens.

The three Italian cruisers had all been firing as they advanced towards the British, but at 1647hrs, they turned to starboard, towards the west-north-west, so that all of their guns could bear on the British cruisers rather than just the forward ones. This also meant the rough swell was coming from astern rather than the port beam, which reduced the rolling of the ships, and so improved the accuracy of their gunnery. At this stage, *Littorio* was on a similar course, 4½ miles astern of the Italian cruisers and 6 miles from Vian's flagship. This was part of Iachino's plan. He fully expected the British Covering Force to put itself between the Italians and the convoy, much as they had done earlier that morning when they were fighting Parona's force. He also expected them to cloak both themselves and the convoy in smoke as they had before.

So, knowing that his force was considerably stronger, Iachino felt he had three options. He had to avoid moving through the smoke, if possible, as that greatly increased the vulnerability of his ships to a surprise torpedo attack. The wind, though, was driving the smoke from the south-east towards the north-west. So, if he turned his command well to the east of the convoy, the smokescreen would be less of a problem. All of his ships, while well-matched to Vian's in terms of speed, were at least twice as fast as the convoy. Therefore, intercepting it shouldn't be a problem, whichever course he took. His second option was to turn west, which increased the interference to visibility caused by the smokescreen but it allowed him to lay his ships across the convoy's path and place his fleet between the convoy and Malta. The third option was to split his force. This, however, weakened his fighting power, and Iachino quickly ruled that out. His decision was to head west with every ship he had and fight it out.

By 1647hrs, the situation had become precarious for Vian. His own cruisers had been heading north to close the range, while Micklethwait's destroyers were somewhere to port of them, wreathed in smoke. *Dido* and *Penelope* were keeping station with *Cleopatra* and *Euryalus*, but were now off the flagship's starboard quarter. All of these British ships were making

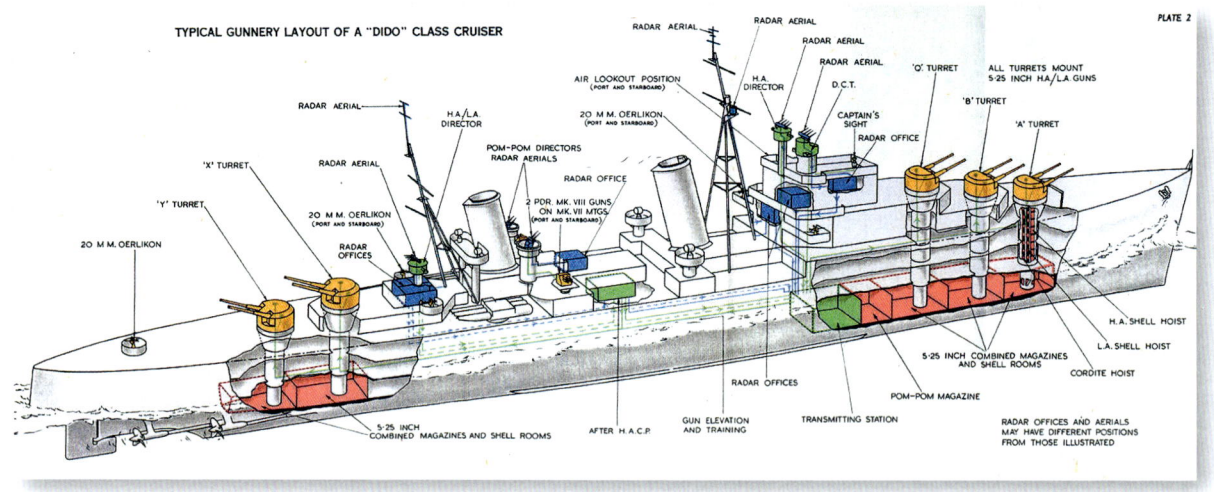

The weapons layout of a British Dido-class AA cruiser. The five twin 5.25in QF gun turrets could engage both air and surface targets, guided by a fire control team based in the Director Control Tower (DCT), and the Transmitting Station below decks. *Cleopatra* and *Dido* carried the Type 281 air warning radar, while *Euryalus* mounted the slightly more effective Type 279 version. In addition, *Euryalus* carried Type 284 (surface) and Type 285 (AA) fire control radars, plus a Type 282 (AA) guiding the 2pdr 'pom-poms', while the other two only carried the Type 285 (AA) set.

smoke as feverishly as they could. When the firing began at 1643hrs, Vian ordered his cruisers to alter course to port and head west, into the thick bank of smoke laid by Micklethwait's destroyers. It would still take a few minutes to reach it and in the meantime, the cruisers were vulnerable. A minute after *Cleopatra* was hit, *Euryalus* was straddled by 15in shells from *Littorio*. Although not hit directly, the cruiser suffered some minor splinter damage as the closest shells exploded on contact with the sea nearby. What probably saved *Euryalus* was the smokescreen being laid by *Cleopatra*, 1,000yds ahead of Capt. Bush's cruiser.

Vian's flagship, leading the way, was almost completely exposed. Still, it seemed to lead a charmed life, and suffered no more damage until it reached the cover of Micklethwait's smokescreen at 1648hrs. By then, the smoke laid by the cruisers was largely blocking them from sight, and *Dido* and *Penelope*, heading west astern of *Euryalus*, reached the smoke largely unscathed. *Penelope* suffered some minor damage from another near miss, and shell splinters knocked out the Type 284 fire control radar. This was a blow as the set allowed *Euryalus* to fire its 6in guns to fire with accuracy at the enemy, regardless of the smoke. Still, for the moment, the British cruisers and destroyers in the cover of the smokescreen were relatively safe.

This, though, came at the cost of not knowing exactly where the enemy was and what it was doing. It also prevented the British from firing back at the Italian cruisers 10 miles to the north with any real chance of inflicting damage. Vian became concerned about the possibility that Iachino might be attempting to reach the convoy by heading to the east of Vian's force. So, at 1655hrs, he ordered his cruisers to reverse course, turning to port to check if Iachino was working his way around the smokescreen to the east. *Dido* and *Penelope* followed, which only left Micklethwait's destroyers standing between the enemy and the convoy. Still, with such a dense smokescreen, Vian hoped the Italians might not notice the move. *Littorio* and the cruisers were still firing into the smoke, but without radar their chances of hitting anything were slim.

Still, when he turned away, Vian had a message sent to Micklethwait in *Sikh*, 5 miles to the west, to turn south, to screen the convoy more effectively if the Italians tried to get around Micklethwait to the west of his smokescreen. At that moment the convoy was about 13 miles to the south of *Cleopatra*.

The bridge crew of HMS *Euryalus*, pictured with guns at maximum elevation, during Vian's dash to the east in mid-afternoon to see if any Italian warships were approaching the convoy from the east, hidden behind the smokescreen laid by Vian's destroyers.

Around the same time, Iachino ordered his ships to cease fire. Instead, he would wait for the smoke to clear, or at least until it was thin enough to let him see what the British were doing. The Italian commander's chance came at 1720hrs, when he could see Micklethwait's line of destroyers heading away from him, 7 miles to the south. At the time, the Italian battleship had its guns trained towards the smokescreen, and *Littorio* was beam on to the British. Less than a minute later, a full salvo of nine 15in guns crashed out.

The first salvo went wide, but part of the battleship's second one straddled the destroyer *Havock*. One of these shells was a very near miss, landing off the starboard beam of the H-class destroyer. Large shrapnel splinters from the exploding shell blew a hole through the hull and wrecked the boiler room behind it. Several of the engineering crew were killed or wounded and with high-pressure steam escaping into the boiler space, it was abandoned. This was a serious blow, as the destroyer's speed was cut in half to just over 16kts. As *Havock* was unable to keep up with the other destroyers, Capt. Micklethwait ordered the destroyer's commander Lt Geoffrey Watkins to detach *Havock* from the formation and join the convoy's Close Escort. That was only the first of several hits the hugely outnumbered destroyers would suffer.

Once *Havock* was sent limping off to the south, Micklethwait led *Sikh*, *Lively* and *Hero* in a turn to starboard, making smoke as they went. His intention was to drive off the harassing Italian warships by launching a spread of torpedoes. The range was really too great though – his destroyers' 21in Mark IX torpedoes had a maximum range of 14,000yds (7 miles) at 35kts, and at that moment *Littorio* and the three Italian cruisers were just over 7 miles away to the north. So, the chances of achieving a hit were virtually non-existent. Micklethwait quickly abandoned the idea, deciding to wait for a better opportunity. Instead he turned his destroyers in a full circle to thicken the smokescreen covering *Havock*'s withdrawal.

The Arethusa-class light cruiser HMS *Penelope*, a survivor of Force K, was commanded by Capt. Angus Nicholl during the battle. Although *Penelope* only mounted six 6in guns in three twin turrets, the gun crews were among the most experienced in the fleet. *Penelope* also carried fire control radar; Type 284 for engaging surface targets and Type 285 for anti-aircraft guns. The cruiser was also fitted with a Type 281 air warning set.

He also had them fire their main guns at the enemy – something that would achieve little but would boost the morale of the British destroyer crews who were fighting back. Surprisingly, some shells landed close to *Littorio*, the temerity of which caused some surprise on the Italian battleship's bridge. Micklethwait then led his destroyers off on a zig-zag course to the south, laying more smoke as he went. By then, the destroyers weren't alone. After turning back to the east, Vian's cruisers had a frustrating time of it. At 1711hrs, *Cleopatra* and *Euryalus* emerged from the smoke to find the sea to the north devoid of the enemy. It was clear Iachino hadn't tried moving around the smokescreen to the east and instead had concentrated everything he had further to the west. So, Vian gave the order to turn back and head towards Micklethwait.

First, though, at 1710hrs, his cruisers had to undergo an air attack from six Ju 88s, which had been circling the area looking for targets. The aircraft bombed from high altitude, and the weaving cruisers managed to avoid all of their bombs. By then, at 1716hrs, Capt. Bush of *Euryalus* signalled the news that the destroyers were running towards the south, so Vian led his cruisers south too, zig-zagging as he went to throw off any more aircraft. At one stage, around 1725hrs, *Dido* and *Penelope* circled to starboard to avoid the other two cruisers during an unexpected change of course. That lack of a radio on board the flagship was proving to be a hazard when it came to moving formations of ships. At 1732hrs, Vian learned by semaphore from *Euryalus* that Micklethwait had spotted the Italians steaming towards the south-west, putting them on a direct course towards the convoy. So, at 1735hrs, Vian turned his four cruisers round to the west on a course that would intercept Micklethwait at around 1800hrs.

By 1740hrs, 20 minutes after *Havock* was hit, Micklethwait's destroyers were steering to the south-west, and as usual they were making smoke. Iachino in *Littorio* was 7 miles to the north, steering towards the south-west, accompanied by his three destroyers and keeping well clear of the smokescreen to the east. Parona's three cruisers were 3 miles astern of *Littorio*, having just turned to follow the flagship. He too was accompanied by his four destroyers. At that point, Vian was 6 miles to the south-east of Micklethwait, steaming west, with four cruisers as well *Zulu* and *Hasty*, which had become detached from the rest of Micklethwait's flotilla at 1703hrs when they accompanied Vian on his reconnaissance run to the east.

An Italian Savoia-Marchetti SM.79 Sparviero medium bomber, being armed with a 17.7in (45cm) Si200 aerial torpedo. Once dropped these weapons had a range of 1½ miles, travelling at 40kts. During the air attacks on the convoy on 22 March, most of these torpedoes were dropped at too great a range to have any chance of hitting a target.

About 4 miles west of Vian was Capt. Poland's flotilla of five destroyers, which were on their way to reinforce the convoy. Meanwhile, the convoy itself and its Close Escort was 8 miles to the south-west of Vian's cruisers and steaming directly away from them.

The convoy's course had been somewhat erratic for much of the afternoon. For the past three hours it had been subjected to a string of air attacks, and the escorts of the Close Escort force were running very short of ammunition. Still, over the past hour these escorts had fought five attacks, at 1650hrs, 1707hrs, 1715hrs, 1720hrs and 1731hrs. In most cases, the assailants were small groups of toss-bombing or torpedo-carrying Ju 88s, flying from airfields in North Africa. In one instance, at 1715hrs, the attackers were six high-flying Italian SM.79 bombers. Along the way, the convoy's close escorts had been laying their own smokescreen, as the ships weaved in and out of it to help throw off their tormentors. Adding to both the smoke and the anti-aircraft fire were *Carlisle* and *Avon Vale*.

However, there seemed to be no let-up in the attacks, and the lack of ammunition on board the escorts made it questionable whether this strong air defence could be maintained. The threat would end at sunset (1858hrs), with complete darkness expected by 1918hrs, but at 1740hrs that afternoon that all still seemed a long way away. However, Capt. Poland's destroyers were on their way to reinforce the escorts and were expected to arrive shortly after 1800hrs. That should, in theory, increase their chance of holding the enemy aircraft off until nightfall. Cdr Jellicoe, commanding the Close Escort, understood that Vian's Covering Force was busy keeping at bay a more powerful Italian battlegroup. So far, the Covering Force had managed to hold off the enemy. However, if they couldn't be kept at bay, and came within gunnery range of the convoy, there was little Jellicoe's little escort destroyers could do to protect their charges.

Meanwhile, the intermittent duel between Iachino's battlegroup and Capt. Micklethwait's destroyer flotilla was continuing as his force ran southwards, laying smoke as it went. The deteriorating weather and increasingly rough seas made gunnery difficult, but the larger Italian ships were more stable and

The engine room of a British warship. These two 'stokers' had to fight their battle in their machinery compartments, with no way of knowing what was happening above decks or when an enemy shell might smash into their ship. To compensate, during action most captains gave a running account of the action by way of the ship's loudspeaker system.

so had a slight edge in what was now almost a full gale. This was countered to some extent by the smokescreen blowing towards the Italians, which made the accurate rangefinding of the destroyers by the Italian gunnery direction teams little more than fleeting. The 4in and 4.7in shells fired by the three British destroyers would be no threat to the battleship, but it would give the British crews the illusion that they were fighting back, and it bought time for the nearly crippled *Havock* to get under way again and to hide in the smoke.

Of the three destroyers, Micklethwait's *Sikh* was the most exposed, as it was the lead ship in the line. *Lively* and *Hero* astern of it were partly shrouded by the lead destroyer's smoke. So, *Littorio*'s gunners concentrated on the speeding Tribal-class destroyer. By then, *Littorio* had the range calculated closely, and from 1744hrs on it fired a succession of well-aimed salvos. At 1748hrs, one of them landed close off the destroyer's starboard side, showering the superstructure with splinters. Close misses from the Italian cruisers did the same to *Lively*, the next destroyer astern of *Sikh*. At that point Capt. Micklethwait was convinced that the next salvo would hit *Sikh* and destroy it. So, he ordered his torpedo crews to launch the two unfired 21in torpedoes in his after launcher. Essentially, for safety reasons, he didn't want the destroyer to be sunk with any torpedoes still remaining in their launchers.

At 1750hrs, when the two-torpedo spread was launched, *Littorio* was 8 miles off the destroyer's starboard quarter. This was beyond the maximum range of the torpedoes, so there was no chance of scoring a hit unless the Italian battleship and its escorts moved closer over the next few minutes. They didn't, and around 1804hrs, the two torpedoes ran out of power and dropped to the seabed, some 2 miles short of their target. By then, the whole tactical situation had changed dramatically. First, the crushing salvo Micklethwait expected never came. Instead, at 1749hrs, *Littorio* trained its guns further aft, to engage a new target that had just appeared at the edge of the smokescreen. Micklethwait and the crew of *Sikh* had been saved by the sudden reappearance of Vian's cruisers.

The Tribal-class destroyer was a little unusual as it was larger and better-armed than Britain's other destroyers designed and built in the late 1930s. It was created in response to the larger destroyers being built by Italy, with a powerful gun-armament of eight 4.7in quick-firing guns. Tribals were dubbed 'gun destroyers' by the Royal Navy.

A gap in the smokescreen 2 miles astern of the three British destroyers revealed the approach from the east of *Cleopatra* followed by *Euryalus*. So far, the Italians still couldn't see *Dido* and *Penelope* 2 miles astern of Vian's flagship or the destroyers *Zulu* and *Hasty*, which were accompanying *Dido*. The odds then, which had been ludicrously short during the duel between the battleship and the destroyers, had just shortened by a fraction. If nothing else it gave Iachino another problem to consider. At the time, *Littorio* had been steaming towards the south-west, followed by *Gorizia*, *Trento* and *Bande Nere*. The accompanying destroyers were a mile or more to the north-west of this battle line and took no active part in what followed.

On sighting *Cleopatra*, the battleship turned slightly to port to shorten the range, while the cruisers behind the flagships remained on their old course. Then the battleship's guns trained on Vian's cruiser. At 1750hrs, *Littorio* opened fire. By contrast, *Cleopatra* had been firing for eight minutes, opening up on *Littorio* at 1742hrs, guided by *Euryalus*, and its fully working Type 284 fire control radar. By then, a makeshift radio mast had been erected on *Cleopatra*, enabling Vian to maintain contact with *Euryalus* and the rest of his force. It was a string of ranging reports radioed from *Euryalus* that enabled Vian to target the enemy through all the smoke. These initial salvos weren't particularly accurate and went unnoticed by the Italians, who assumed they had come from the enemy destroyers. Vian had no real intention of engaging in a stand-up duel with the battleship. Instead, he intended to drive *Littorio* off using torpedoes.

At 1759hrs, Vian signalled Capt. Poland in *Jervis*, ordering his flotilla to reverse course and then head north towards Micklethwait's three destroyers. Once there, he would close with the Italian battleship, and when in range his six destroyers would launch a massed torpedo attack. Even if it wasn't successful, at least it should force *Littorio* to turn away, and so gain time for the convoy to escape. Until Poland appeared, Vian had to keep *Littorio* fully occupied. At 1802hrs, as *Cleopatra* emerged completely from the smokescreen, Vian caught sight of the battleship about 13,000yds (6½ miles) to the north-west. *Cleopatra* immediately turned to port, to skirt the edge

The crew of the J, K & N class destroyer HMS *Kimberley*, pictured in relaxed and casual 'rig' during a surprise visit from Prime Minister Winston Churchill to the ship in the summer of 1944. In the foreground is one of the destroyer's 21in torpedo launchers, on its quintruple mounting abaft the funnel. At Second Sirte, *Kimberley*'s sister ship HMS *Kelvin* launched four of its five torpedoes from its identical launcher – the fifth one malfunctioned.

of the smokescreen, heading south. Then the cruiser opened up with its ten 5.25in guns. Astern of the flagship, still in the smoke, *Euryalus* was also shooting at *Littorio* using fire control radar. Further astern and deeper into the smoke, *Dido* and *Penelope* both lacked working fire control radars and so held their fire.

Then, at 1805hrs, as the battleship's 15in salvos were landing nearby, *Cleopatra*'s torpedo officer declared the starboard torpedo launcher was trained and ready. The order was given and at 1806hrs, three 21in Mark IX torpedoes left their triple launcher and set off towards *Littorio*. At that point the range was about 12,000yds (6 miles), which was just within the maximum range of these torpedoes. However, at 30kts, it would take 24 minutes for them to reach the battleship. Their only chance of hitting *Littorio* was if it didn't change course and the torpedo officer's angle of launch was the right one. This, though, was meant to be nothing more than a distraction. When Poland's destroyer flotilla arrived, a full-scale torpedo attack would be made. At that moment, the flotilla was racing north, and was still 3 miles to the south of Vian, close to Micklethwait's battered flotilla.

After the torpedoes left their launcher, Vian ordered his cruisers to turn hard to port and to reverse course, back into the smoke. He wanted to save his cruisers from harm and returning into the cover of the smoke was the best way to protect them. As *Cleopatra* and *Euryalus* turned, still under heavy fire from *Littorio*, they began laying yet more black funnel smoke. Before they were lost from sight, at 1806hrs, a final salvo from *Littorio*'s secondary battery landed close to *Cleopatra* and shell splinters scythed into the cruiser's open bridge, causing several casualties. Capt. Guy Grantham and R. Adm. Vian were both unhurt. Just before the battered cruiser disappeared again into the smoke, Vian was able to notice something that might prove useful.

The three enemy cruisers were now 2 miles behind the battleship and heading off on a slightly different course. So, apart from its small destroyer escort, *Littorio* was all alone.

Vian's primary concern was the safety of the convoy. It was currently only 6 miles to the south of him. Without all the smoke, it might have been visible to the lookouts on board *Littorio*. The increasingly rough seas were causing problems, with some wave crests up to 4m (13ft) high, and the Italian ships were beam on to what was fast becoming a south-easterly gale. As for visibility, the British official report after the battle described visibility that afternoon as 'patchy and deteriorating'. The smoke made it much worse. That meant Vian had to keep the smokescreen going, if possible, and to keep *Littorio* from falling on the convoy.

Certainly, at that stage of the battle, *Littorio* posed the most serious threat to the convoy. Its four merchant ships were now just 11 miles to the south-east of the battleship, and on a parallel course. Visibility was probably less than 8 miles at this stage, but the convoy was still within range of *Littorio*'s guns. So, at 1805hrs, just as the torpedoes were being launched, Vian ordered the convoy to turn south again, and so move further away from the enemy battleship. He sensed that the climax of this peculiar running battle was approaching. With sunset at 1858hrs that evening, Vian knew he still had an hour to go before darkness started cloaking the convoy. In that time, he expected Iachino to make a determined lunge towards the convoy. So, Vian had to be prepared for a lunge of his own, to keep the Italians at bay until nightfall.

'THE MEDINA MELEE'

In a way, Vian's flagship had already upset any plans Iachino had made. At 1811hrs, lookouts in *Littorio* spotted torpedo tracks in the water and the battleship turned slightly to starboard, onto a westerly course. This way, even if the torpedoes did reach them, the battleship should be able to thread through them. In the end, the change of course, and therefore the greater distance from the torpedo's firing point, ensured that *Cleopatra*'s torpedo salvo missed its mark. However, by 1820hrs, *Littorio* turned to the south-west again, in its bid to move around the smoke and to get ahead of the slower-moving convoy. The smokescreen was now about 6 miles away from the Italians, despite Micklethwait's attempts to extend it further towards the south-west. That was what his three destroyers had been doing since *Littorio* stopped targeting them.

At 1820hrs, Vian turned back to the west, leading his four cruisers and attached destroyers back into the smoke. At that moment, Micklethwait's destroyers were 3 miles away, busily laying smoke, while Poland's five destroyers were close by, heading north, having reached the safety of Micklethwait's smokescreen. Poland's destroyers were making smoke as well, to cloak their approach. Having been ordered to carry out a flotilla torpedo attack, Poland swung his line of destroyers round to the west, with his flotilla leader *Jervis* leading, followed by *Kingston*, *Kipling*, *Kelvin* and *Legion*. He also ordered them to increase speed to 34kts. This was dangerous with a gale blowing from astern, but utterly necessary if they were to survive the next few minutes.

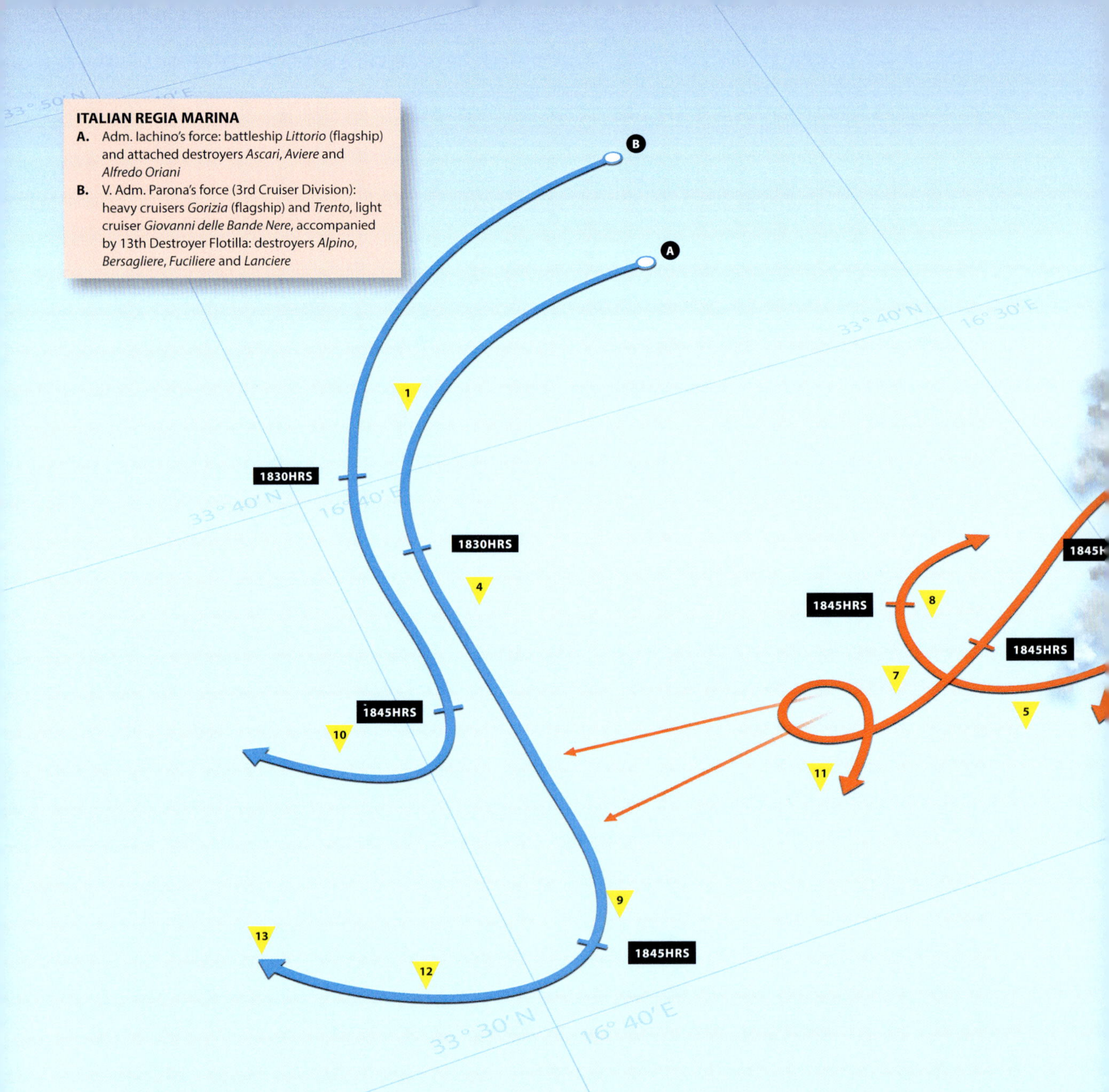
ITALIAN REGIA MARINA
A. Adm. Iachino's force: battleship Littorio (flagship) and attached destroyers Ascari, Aviere and Alfredo Oriani
B. V. Adm. Parona's force (3rd Cruiser Division): heavy cruisers Gorizia (flagship) and Trento, light cruiser Giovanni delle Bande Nere, accompanied by 13th Destroyer Flotilla: destroyers Alpino, Bersagliere, Fuciliere and Lanciere
B
A
1
1830HRS
1830HRS
4
1845HRS
8
1845HRS
7
1845HRS
5
1845HRS
10
11
9
13
12
1845HRS
33° 40' N
16° 30' E
33° 30' N
16° 40' E

EVENTS

1. 1820hrs: Adm. Iachino turns *Littorio* to the south-west, then due south, in an attempt to push past R. Adm. Vian's Covering Force and reach the convoy.

2. 1820hrs: Vian turns west, while ordering his two destroyer flotillas to support each other and place themselves between the Italians and the convoy.

3. 1828hrs: Capt. Micklethwait of 22nd Destroyer Flotilla is ordered to lay more smoke, extending the smokescreen to the south-west.

4. 1832hrs: Lookouts in *Littorio* and the Italian cruisers spot the approach of Capt. Poland's 14th Destroyer Flotilla from the south-east.

5. 1834hrs: Capt. Poland in destroyer *Jervis* sights *Littorio* and deploys his five destroyers in line abreast before launching a high-speed attack.

6. 1840hrs: Vian's cruisers *Cleopatra* and *Euryalus* sight *Littorio* and open fire on the battleship. The Italians return fire and *Euryalus* is damaged by a near miss.

7. 1841hrs: Destroyer *Kingston* is hit by a shell and is disabled and brought to a stop. A minute later, Poland orders his remaining destroyers to turn to starboard and launch their torpedoes. In all, 17 torpedoes are fired, including three from the stricken *Kingston*.

8. 1842hrs: Poland's flotilla then turns away, making smoke. Meanwhile Micklethwait's 22nd Destroyer Flotilla advance to protect *Kingston* with smoke and cover the withdrawal of the 14th Destroyer Flotilla.

9. 1842hrs: Iachino orders *Littorio* to turn away from the approaching torpedoes and withdraw to the north-west. The battleship continues to fire on the British warships.

10. 1843hrs: Parona's cruisers copy *Littorio*'s manoeuvre and turn simultaneously towards the north-west, while also maintaining a steady fire from their rear turrets.

11. 1851hrs: Destroyer *Lively* is damaged by a near miss from a 15in shell, but still manages to launch torpedoes at the Italians as they withdraw.

12. 1852hrs: Both sides are still firing at each other, despite the fading light, and a glow on *Littorio*'s stern is regarded as a possible hit by the British. In fact, it was the battleship's floatplane catching fire, following the blast of the battleship's own guns.

13. 1855hrs: Iachino orders his ships to cease fire and by 1856hrs, both sides have stopped firing. This effectively brings the battle to an end.

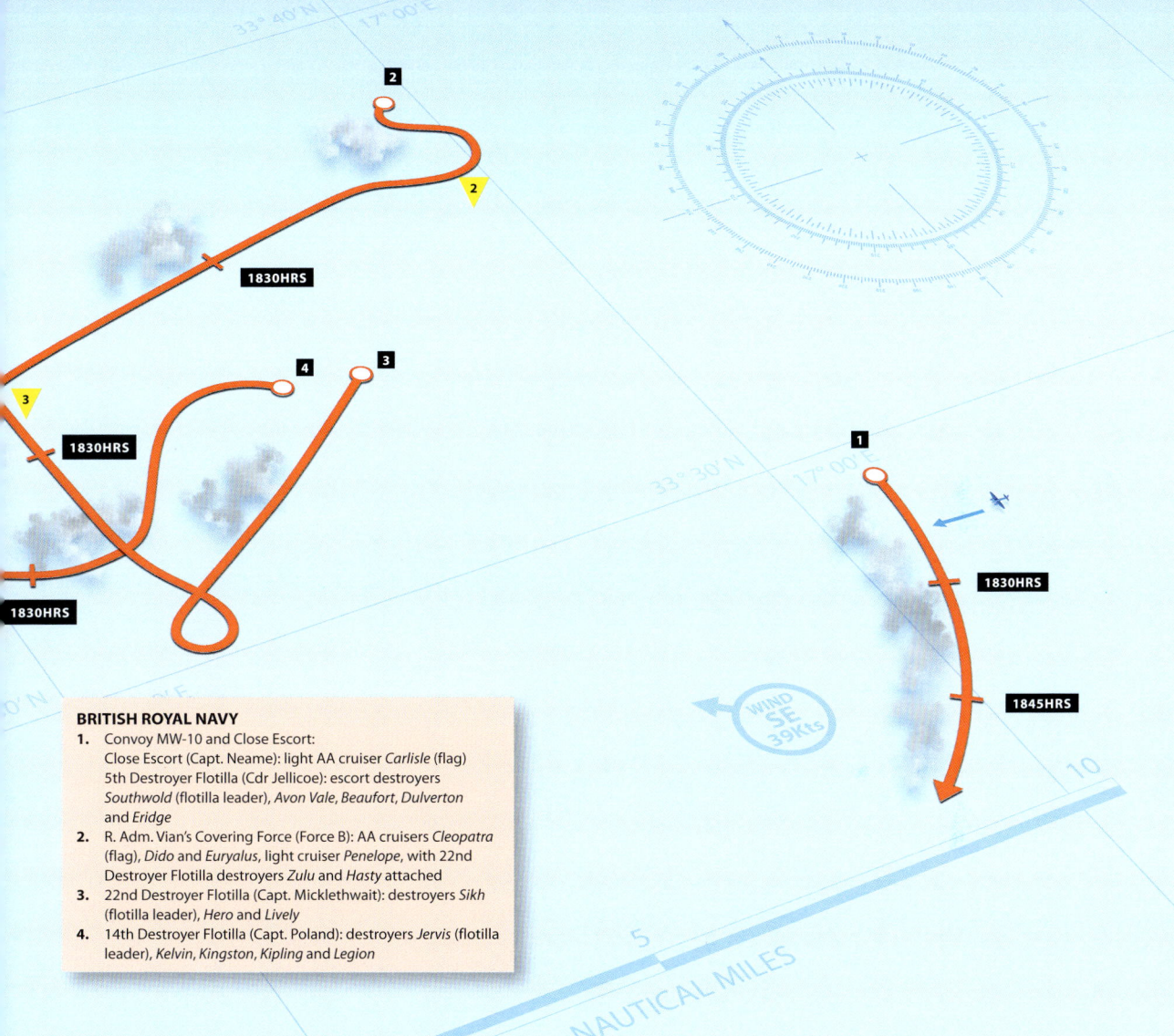

BRITISH ROYAL NAVY
1. Convoy MW-10 and Close Escort:
   Close Escort (Capt. Neame): light AA cruiser *Carlisle* (flag)
   5th Destroyer Flotilla (Cdr Jellicoe): escort destroyers *Southwold* (flotilla leader), *Avon Vale*, *Beaufort*, *Dulverton* and *Eridge*
2. R. Adm. Vian's Covering Force (Force B): AA cruisers *Cleopatra* (flag), *Dido* and *Euryalus*, light cruiser *Penelope*, with 22nd Destroyer Flotilla destroyers *Zulu* and *Hasty* attached
3. 22nd Destroyer Flotilla (Capt. Micklethwait): destroyers *Sikh* (flotilla leader), *Hero* and *Lively*
4. 14th Destroyer Flotilla (Capt. Poland): destroyers *Jervis* (flotilla leader), *Kelvin*, *Kingston*, *Kipling* and *Legion*

'THE MEDINA MELEE', 1815–1855HRS, 22 MARCH 1942

By 1815hrs, with sunset less than 40 minutes away, Adm. Iachino was running out of time. If he was to intercept the convoy he needed to brush past R. Adm. Vian's Covering Force and push south. Smoke still screened the British ships, but whenever the British emerged from it, Iachino's ships concentrated their fire on the enemy warships. Then, at 1837hrs, everything changed. Captain Poland's 14th Destroyer Flotilla sighted *Littorio* and deployed for a massed torpedo attack. Afterwards, the participants called this fight 'The Medina Melee'. In reality, it was a highly risky enterprise, five destroyers taking on a battleship amid the teeth of a gale. While this daring action didn't result in any torpedo hits, it forced Iachino to turn away and so give up his last chance to destroy the convoy.

This photograph taken from HMS *Jervis* captures the moment when the destroyer following astern, HMS *Kelvin*, emerged from the smokescreen screening Convoy MW-10. At that moment, *Kelvin* began a high-speed torpedo attack on the Italian battleship *Littorio* amid rough, rolling seas and a strengthening gale. In these circumstances the poor quality of the hasty shot can be forgiven.

All the destroyers were beginning to suffer from the gale hitting them from astern, with seas washing over their decks, rails and boats being smashed and the crew closed up at action stations being covered by sheets of flying spray. Then, at 1834hrs, as *Jervis* turned to the north to try and see through the spray, its bridge lookouts spotted the battleship, 18,000yds (9 miles) away to the north-west, on a bearing of 282°. Poland immediately gave the order for all of the ships to turn west, into a line abreast formation, and begin their high-speed torpedo run. Afterwards, the destroyer crews dubbed this extremely risky attack 'The Medina Melee'. By this stage, *Littorio* had altered course again, this time to the south, in a determined bid to reach the convoy before dark. Behind the battleship, Parona's three cruisers followed in line, with all the ships spaced a mile apart from each other. Strangely, due to the conditions, Poland spotted the second cruiser, *Trento*, at 1837hrs, five full minutes before the rest of the Italian ships were seen.

The Italians, with the advantage of height and stability, spotted the approaching destroyers at 1832hrs. Soon Poland's ships came under a heavy fire, both from the battleship and the cruisers, with 15in, 8in and 6in shells all heading towards Poland's speeding destroyers. However, a combination of the smoke, which the destroyers were just emerging from, and the rough seas all reduced the accuracy of this fire, and no hits were made at this point. Poland was able to press home his attack, and with *Littorio* remaining on a southerly course, the range dropped rapidly. The salvos from the Italian guns continued to fall close by the destroyers. The destroyers were firing back too, although this was more for the benefit of the British gun crews than anything else, who wanted to play their part in the drama.

By early 1942 the destroyer HMS *Hero*, a veteran of Narvik (1940), had been in the Mediterranean for almost two years and had seen extensive action. At Sirte, Cdr Ralph Fisher was temporarily in command for the venture, as the destroyer's usual captain, Cdr Hilary Biggs, had fallen ill. *Hero* was the only British warship in Force B without radar.

In fact, it wasn't just the British destroyers that were under fire. At 1840hrs, when the torpedo attack was reaching its climax, *Cleopatra* and *Euryalus* had emerged from the smokescreen, just to the north-east of the charging destroyers, and were lending the weight of their fire, targeting *Littorio* at a range of 12,000yds (6 miles). To their right, *Hero*, *Lively* and *Sikh* were still busy extending the smokescreen, giving Vian's cruisers better cover. Sure enough, *Littorio*'s main guns trained aft and opened fire on the cruisers. Although no hits were scored, at 1841hrs, a near miss caused substantial splinter damage to *Euryalus*, peppering the cruiser's upperworks amidships on the port side. The cruisers remained in place, as Vian was determined to support Poland as much as he could during his torpedo attack.

On board *Jervis*, Lt John Moss described his role during the torpedo run:

> My action station was on the plot. I was passed ranges and bearings of the enemy when visible and kept an estimated track of his movement when he was hidden by smoke. At speed and in rough weather there was a lot of vibration, and once, when we fired a broadside all the lights went out, including the projection compass rose on the underside of the glass table. There were frantic demands thro' the bridge voice-pipe for enemy movements, and we had to improvise with a torch!

His job was crucial, as with a closing speed of more than a thousand yards a minute, Poland needed to know the exact time to launch his torpedo attack. The British 21in Mark IX torpedo had a maximum range of 11,000yds at 36kts, or 14,000yds at 30kts. Poland opted for the slower, longer-ranged setting, to increase the chances of hitting something.

As they made their approach, the destroyer crews could barely see the battleship ahead of them through the spray and rough seas, and through the salvos erupting around them. Astern of *Littorio*, they eventually made out all three of the Italian cruisers, which were following the battleship in line astern. It was a heady moment, this rush towards the battleship at 30kts, in a following gale. With so many shells erupting around them, it seemed a

THE TORPEDO ATTACK ON THE BATTLESHIP *LITTORIO*, 1841HRS, 22 MARCH 1942 (PP.76–77)

By 1759hrs it was clear to R. Adm. Vian that the Italians were now trying force their way past his Covering Force to the west, in a last attempt to reach the convoy before nightfall. Leading the way was Adm. Iachino in his flagship, the battleship *Littorio*. Vian therefore ordered his destroyers to prepare to launch a massed torpedo attack on the battleship. At 1834hrs, Capt. Poland's destroyer flotilla emerged from the smokescreen and spotted *Littorio* 9 miles to the west. On Poland's order the five destroyers fanned out, with his flotilla leader HMS *Jervis* (**1**) the most northerly of them. Off the port beam were HMS *Kipling* (**2**) and HMS *Kelvin* (**3**), with HMS *Kingston* and HMS *Legion* further to the south. The destroyers then raced towards the battleship, making 32kts, despite the now gale force seas and strong winds hitting them from astern (**4**). *Littorio* and the Italian cruisers astern of the battleship opened fire on the destroyers racing towards them from the east (**5**), but amazingly only *Kingston* was hit, at 1841hrs, when the destroyer was struck by an 8in shell fired by *Gorizia*. Afterwards, though, the crippled destroyer was able to limp away. This shows the scene just before *Kingston* was hit. A minute later, Poland gave the order for the flotilla to swing to starboard and launch their torpedoes at a range of 3 miles.

A fast convoy from Alexandria to Malta in early 1942, pictured from the bridge of the destroyer HMS *Kelvin*. Cdr John Allison's destroyer took part in 'The Medina Melee', launching four of its five torpedoes at *Littorio*. However, two were fired prematurely, as Allison's bridge team mistook the signal to 'turn to run in' for one signalling 'fire'. The following month, Cdr Allison was replaced and sent home to take up a shore appointment.

suicidal undertaking. However, for the most part, Capt. Poland and his men were lucky. At 1841hrs, *Kingston* was hit by a shell from either *Littorio*'s 6in battery or from *Gorizia* with its 8in guns. To this day it remains unclear which Italian ship scored the hit. The shell smashed into the ship's whaler stowed under the searchlight platform, wrecking both before exploding near the torpedo tubes, and blowing a large smoking hole in the destroyer's deck.

The explosion ripped into one of the destroyer's boiler rooms, which was set ablaze. The engine room astern of it was also flooded. One of the survivors, Gunner Bill Davidson, recalled the carnage, 'I was a gunlayer [at the 3in AA gun just aft of the searchlight tower] and shrapnel entered under my legs, killing two of my crew, and injuring the other two. I was the only gun crew member unharmed.' In all, 15 of *Kingston*'s crew were killed. The destroyer

The Italian flagship *Littorio* pictured in the camouflage scheme the battleship used during the battle. During the fight, its 15in (38.1cm) guns fired 181 rounds at Vian's force, and a further 445 rounds were fired from the secondary 6in (15.2cm) port side battery.

In most British destroyers, a torpedo team of around a dozen operated the torpedo tubes, led by a junior officer and a petty officer. In the Mediterranean, these young men rarely had the chance to fire their weapons in anger. At Second Sirte, though, the torpedo teams of most of the two British destroyer flotillas were finally given their moment. Although no hits were scored, they successfully forced the Italian battlefleet to break off the action, and so these torpedo teams helped save the convoy.

was stopped dead in the water, but somehow Lt Cdr Philip Somerville managed to turn the destroyer to starboard despite the gale slamming into the damaged ship from astern. Rolling dangerously, *Kingston* remained there long enough for the torpedo crew to pull away the dead and wounded, and then add their own four torpedoes to Capt. Poland's flotilla-sized spread.

The destroyer then turned into the gale and remained there, wallowing helplessly, until Vian spotted their predicament and led his cruisers towards the crippled destroyer. They swaddled *Kingston* in a thick smokescreen, and eventually the battle moved on. That evening, Somerville and his men were able to put out the fire, contain the flooding, tend to the dead and wounded and then finally limp away under their one remaining engine, making 16kts. Then, as Davidson put it, 'We managed to get one engine going and managed to crawl into Malta under our own steam.' Even that was a feat in itself, in the teeth of a fully-blown gale. However, during the torpedo run, the crippling of *Kingston* didn't stop the attack. The hit on *Kingston* took place during the final moments of the approach, just seconds before Poland gave the order to turn to the north and unleash the torpedoes.

During the approach run, Able Seaman John Ellis of *Jervis* knew nothing about their target. Afterwards, he recalled, 'As we came through the smoke I asked the officer at our gun, "What is that great big thing?" He replied "a Littorio class battleship!" What a shock!' The destroyers ran a gauntlet of fire as they raced towards the battleship. Ellis didn't describe the torpedo attack, but his diary contained a montage of events on board the destroyer

British torpedo attack, 1834–1844hrs, 22 March 1942

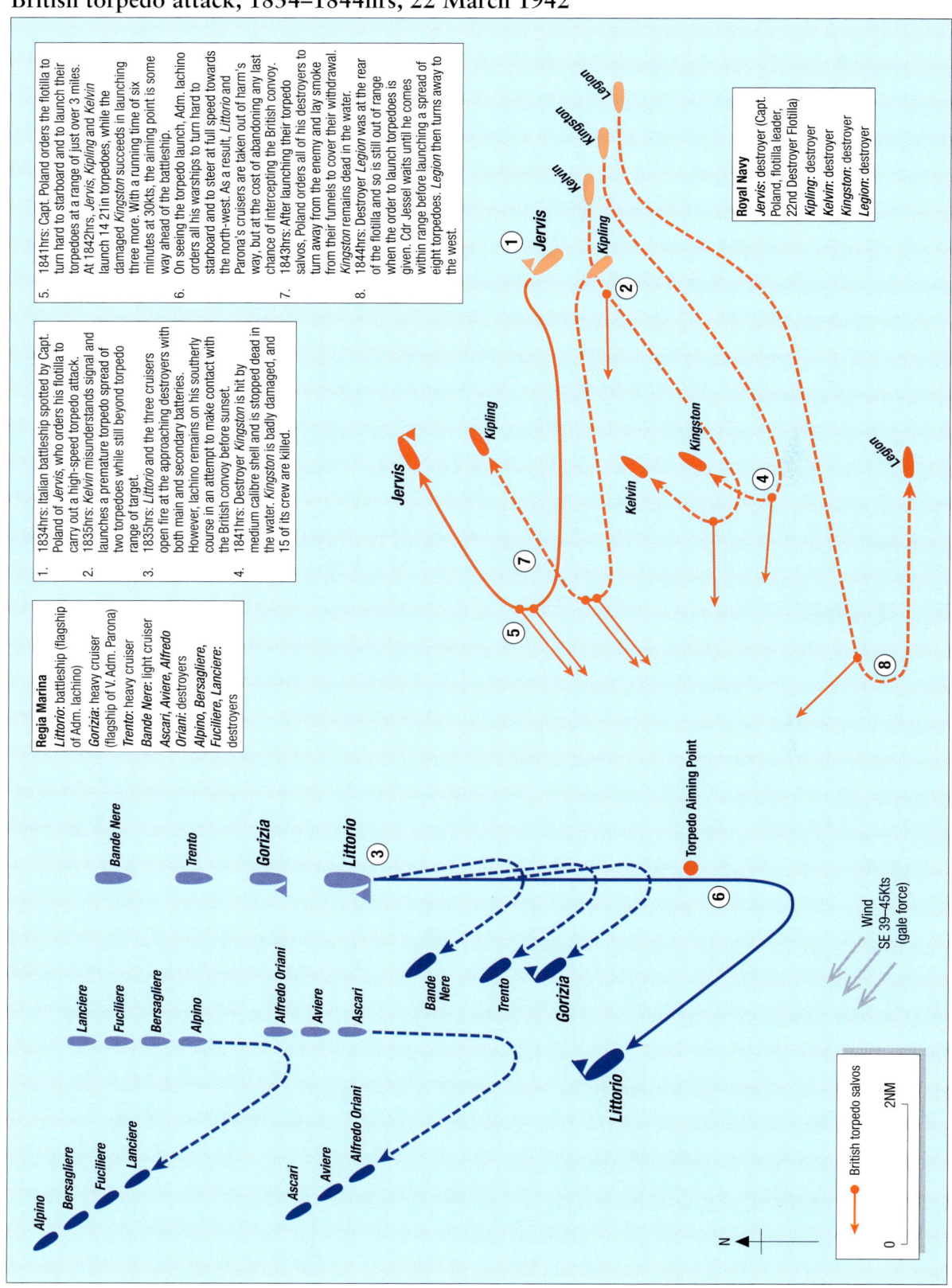

while it happened: 'During the action the ship's tabby cat had kittens in the wardroom, and for some reason she insists on carrying them onto the upper deck. *Kingston*, second in line, is damaged. Our No. 1 gun shield is battered in […] all the guardrails and several washdeck lockers are swept over the side. Motor cutter shattered, and upside down in her davits.'

The four destroyers continued their high-speed attack until Poland decided they were close enough to launch their torpedoes. On board *Jervis*, Lt Moss was watching the range close, and updating Poland on the rapidly shrinking distance. At a speed of 34kts, the destroyers were closing at the rate of more than 1,100yds a minute. So, the entire torpedo run, from emerging from the smokescreen to reaching the launch point took no more than 12 minutes. For those on the destroyers' bridges, though, it must have seemed an eternity. Finally, when Moss reported the range was down to just 6,000yds, Poland made his move. Three miles from the battleship, on Poland's order, the remaining destroyers turned hard to starboard, to present their full torpedo broadside.

At 1842hrs, the torpedoes were sent on their way. *Legion*, struggling through the seas at the south end of the line, had to creep closer, and launched its torpedoes two minutes later. Each boat carried a single launcher mounting five torpedo tubes. When built, these destroyers carried twice the number, but by early 1942, all of those in Poland's flotilla had had their after torpedo launcher removed and replaced by a 4in Mark V anti-aircraft gun of the kind crewed by Gunner Davidson of *Kingston*. In *Legion*, attached for the day from Force K, its after quadruple launcher had been replaced in the same way.

In theory, Poland's destroyers had 24 torpedoes available. In the end, only 17 were launched, as some tubes had been damaged during the approach or simply malfunctioned. Due to a problem with the launcher, *Kelvin* also expended two torpedoes prematurely, at 1835hrs, before the enemy battleship was in range. Still, it was a dangerous torpedo spread for the Italians, spread out in a swathe over a mile wide.

The destroyer HMS *Kingston*, as the ship appeared when first commissioned, two weeks into the war. During 'The Medina Melee', *Kingston* was hit by a shell from *Littorio* or *Gorizia* and was disabled. However, Cdr Philip Somerville's crew managed to get the destroyer under way again, and *Kingston* limped into Malta. However, *Kingston* was bombed repeatedly while in Malta and several of the crew were killed, including Somerville. On 11 April, *Kingston* sank in dock, after taking a direct hit from a bomb dropped by a Ju 87 Stuka.

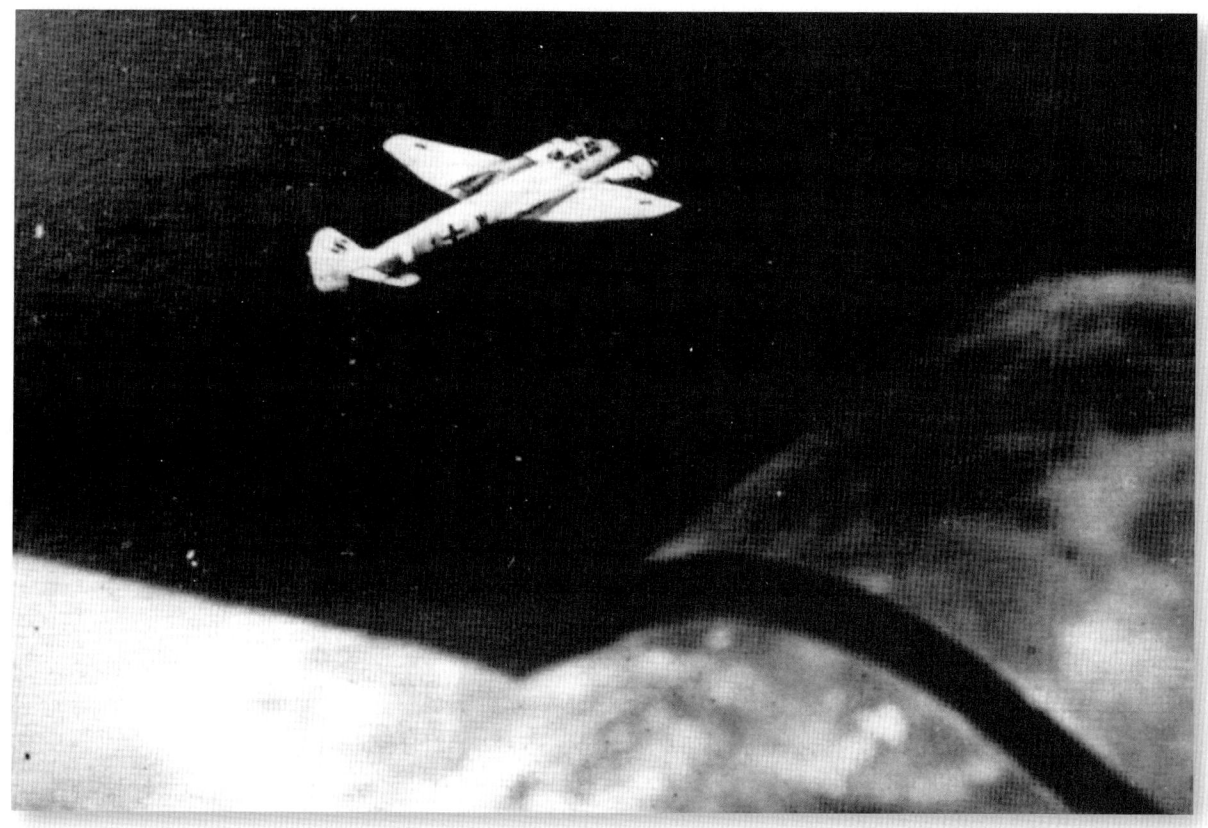

A German Junkers Ju 88A twin-engined bomber, pictured from another aircraft in its *staffel* (unit or squadron), during air operations over the central Mediterranean in 1942. These bombers were the offensive mainstay of Fliegerkorps X, which in the spring of 1942 operated from airfields in Crete, Greece and Cyrenaica.

On the Admiral's Bridge of *Littorio*, Iachino and his officers watched the destroyers swing to the north, then loose the torpedoes. Although nobody could be sure of the capabilities of the British ordnance, the torpedo performance would be broadly similar to the Italian 21in 'Naples' torpedo, so the torpedoes would probably have a speed of 30–36kts. That meant that if he maintained his southerly course, he could expect to pass into the area encompassed by the torpedo spread in the next 10–12 minutes. The battleship was protected by the Pugliese torpedo defence system, but it wasn't worth putting it to the test against so many torpedoes. It was too great a risk. So, at 1842hrs, Iachino ordered Capt. Bacigalupi to turn away from the threat, and to increase speed in an attempt to outrun the torpedoes. Bacigalupi gave the order, and *Littorio* turned to starboard, onto a north-westerly course.

The two sides were still shooting at each other at this stage, although the battleship's change of course amid the increasingly rough sea conditions made gunnery extremely challenging. Still, at 1851hrs, just before *Littorio* turned a little more to the north, a hit was scored on the destroyer *Lively*, 5 miles to the east of the battleship. Micklethwait's three destroyers turned towards *Kingston* after the destroyer was hit, laying smoke as they went. Vian's cruisers were doing the same, but *Littorio* targeted the smoke-laying destroyers, as he feared another torpedo attack, either against *Littorio* or on Parona's cruisers, which had also turned away to the north-west. He was right to be concerned. Capt. Micklethwait saw the Italians turn away and decided to give chase, launching another torpedo attack, this time from the starboard side of the withdrawing battleship.

Micklethwait turned *Sikh* towards the north-west at high speed. However, at 1851hrs, he ordered the launch of another torpedo spread, but in the smoke and spray, *Sikh* and *Hero* couldn't see the target. Anyway, given the bearing, a hit on the target was impossible. *Lively*, though, was willing and able to launch a full spread of eight Mark IX torpedoes. The range was 8,000yds (4 miles), but the angle was poor as the Italian ships were steaming away from the destroyer. In the end, as with Poland's larger spread a few minutes earlier, all the torpedoes missed. A few seconds after firing, *Lively* was bracketed by a salvo of 15in shells fired from *Littorio*. A near miss showered the destroyer with splinter damage. One piece pierced its hull, and severed a steam line, which reduced the destroyers' speed to 17kts. Micklethwait immediately detached *Lively* and ordered Lt Cdr William Eyre-Hussey to head directly for Tobruk, 360 miles away in North Africa, for immediate repairs.

This little action had another consequence for the Italians. As they pursued the Italians, the three British destroyers fired at *Littorio*, when they could see it amid the rough seas. At that point, the battleship was directly to the west of them. *Littorio* was firing too; it was one of these three-gun salvos fired from its rear turret that damaged *Lively*. At 1852hrs, a glow was seen on the battleship's stern. Hopes were raised that either a torpedo had struck the battleship, or else one of the salvos from the British destroyers had scored an unlikely hit. In fact, it turned out to be a self-inflicted wound. The blast of *Littorio*'s after turret had damaged its Ro.43 floatplane, mounted at the stern, and the biplane had caught fire.

This proved to be the last exchange of the battle. At 1855hrs, as visibility made the British difficult to see, Iachino gave the order to cease fire. At that moment, Vian's cruisers were heading towards the south-west, so they could protect the convoy if the enemy tried to hunt it down again. Poland's destroyers had withdrawn to the east, making smoke, while Micklethwait's, after their torpedo launch, turned to starboard and headed towards Vian's flagship. The convoy, 8 miles to the south-east of Vian, was still heading towards the south-west, and making good progress now that the air attacks had stopped. So, despite the fading light and mounting seas, Vian's battered command was still intact, and willing to continue the fight until nightfall.

Iachino, however, had decided to call off the attack. He continued to withdraw his ships towards the north-north-west, in the general direction of his base at Taranto, 350 miles away. Darkness was coming, and as the nocturnal ambush of the Italian cruisers at the Battle of Matapan a year earlier had shown, the British were greatly superior in night operations. After all, they had trained extensively in nighttime gunnery, while the Italians had largely ignored this facet of naval operations. The night was especially dangerous for the Italians as the British had radar and they didn't. So, with a storm brewing, Iachino headed for home. He was reasonably content. After all, despite not having stopped the convoy, thanks to Vian's dogged defence of it, he had delayed it considerably. Now, it would be up to Axis aircraft to finish the job.

THE FINAL LEG

The final shots of the battle had been fired at 1856hrs. Darkness had almost completely descended, and five minutes before, Adm. Iachino had

The British 4.7in quick-firing gun was mounted in the Tribal, G, H & I and J, K & N classes of destroyers that made up the two flotillas which took part in the battle. The Mark XII twin mounting shown here is from a Tribal class vessel. These manually operated guns had a rate of fire of around 10rpm and an effective range of eight miles.

set a course towards the north-east, and Taranto. It had been almost an hour since the last air attack on the convoy, and it seemed that all of the Axis bombers in the air were on their way back to Cyrenaica. As night settled, it gradually became clear that the long, hard-fought battle was over. On board *Cleopatra*, Vian's flag officer, Capt. Grantham, was still unconvinced it was all done with: 'I had forgotten to wind my watch the night before, and the day seemed endless. When we were getting low on ammunition, I looked at my watch, and said to the Admiral, "I don't think we have enough rounds to last until dark".' In fact, as he spoke, nightfall was less than 30 minutes away.

As the Italians withdrew, Vian gathered his Covering Force together, and headed towards the south-west, towards the convoy, which was 10 miles away. At 1940hrs, before the two forces made contact, Vian made the decision to adhere to his plan, to withdraw the Covering Force and return to Alexandria. There was little likelihood that the Italian battlefleet would return and attempt a night attack. With his warships running low on fuel and the sea conditions deteriorating, it was imperative not to delay the recall of his force. Meanwhile, the convoy would continue to Malta, through

The MV *Pampas* was one of the four merchant vessels that made up Convoy MW-10. The 15,500-ton British-flagged vessel made it into Valletta on the morning of 23 March, despite having been hit by two bombs that failed to explode. However, the ship was bombed and sunk three days later, before most of the cargo on board could be unloaded. In this photograph of the convoy at sea, *Pampas* is in the foreground with the Norwegian-registered M/S *Talabot* off its starboard beam.

the night, at best possible speed. Its Close Escort of Cdr Jellicoe's escort destroyers was also low on fuel and so needed to reach Malta, where they could replenish.

Meanwhile, at 1900hrs, in line with his own operational orders, the Convoy Commodore ordered the four ships of the convoy to disperse. The intent was that by sending the merchantmen off on diverging courses, dawn would find them spread out over a score of miles of sea. Then, each would head towards Malta, escorted by one or two escort destroyers. In retrospect, maintaining formation would have offered them a better collective chance of reaching Valletta, but then the whole convoy would have become the target of everything the Luftwaffe in Sicily could throw against them. Afterwards, Hutchinson wrote, 'My plan for dispersal was based on the speed of the ships. Thus, *Clan Campbell* being the slowest, was to proceed direct ... *Talabot*, *Pampas* and *Breconshire* were to make legs to the southward ... the amount of diversion depending on the speed of the ships.' He added, 'The idea was, that by daylight on Monday, March 23rd the convoy would again be concentrated, and in the swept channel ...'

Meanwhile, in Alexandria, Adm. Cunningham had been following the course of the battle and was relieved that darkness had fallen. On hearing of Vian's plans to withdraw on schedule, Cunningham ordered that AA cruiser HMS *Carlisle* accompany the convoy into Malta to boost its defence. Vian had already intended to detach *Penelope* and *Legion*, but he now decided to detach *Havock* and *Kingston* as well, as they were too damaged to return to Alexandria, especially when sailing into the teeth of a gale. Once these ships were detached, at 2000hrs, Vian's Covering Force – now designated Force B again – turned about, and set off back to Malta, amid what would soon amount to storm-force seas.

The same storm buffeted the dispersed convoy and its remaining scattering escorts. Sunrise at 0600hrs on D+3 (Monday 23 March) revealed grey, overcast skies and very rough seas. The conditions had delayed the four merchant ships as they separately headed towards Malta. The plan was to

The light cruiser HMS *Penelope* pictured while attempting to tow the damaged auxiliary supply ship HMS *Breconshire* into Valletta on the morning of Monday 23 March. The attempt was thwarted by the gale-force winds and rough seas, and instead, *Breconshire* was anchored in Marsaxlokk Bay, on the south-east side of Malta.

converge at the southern end of the swept channel through the minefields that led into Valletta's Grand Harbour. Originally, this had been expected to be reached by mid-morning. Instead, as the convoy had been pushed to the south of its planned track and had been delayed by the dispersal and then by the weather conditions, this wasn't possible. So, the ships were exposed to air attacks for longer than had been expected.

The real problem was that at dawn Axis bombers had arrived over the island and began pounding Malta's airfields. As a result, the air cover Capt. Hutchinson expected never appeared as the fighters couldn't take off. So, apart from a few escorts, the merchantmen were left to their own devices. The masters of the Norwegian-flagged M/S *Talabot* and MV *Pampas* decided to cut through the Italian minefield, rather than steam around it towards the swept channel. This drastic measure would shave an hour off the voyage. They made it, although at 0835hrs, they were both attacked by Ju 88s. Their bombs missed *Talabot*, which made it into harbour unscathed shortly after 0900hrs. A few miles astern of the Norwegian freighter, *Pampas* was struck by two bombs, but these turned out to be duds and didn't explode. *Pampas* made it safely into the harbour a little before 1000hrs.

That left HMS *Breconshire*, commanded by the Convoy Commodore, and SS *Clan Campbell*, the engines of which were causing trouble again and so the freighter had lagged far behind the others. *Breconshire* had been under air attack since 0720hrs, but the ship had three escort destroyers positioned around it, ahead and off the port and starboard beams. Meanwhile, *Carlisle* circled around this one-ship convoy, lending its weight to the repeated low-level bomb attacks by Ju 88s. At the same time, the bombing of Malta's airfields continued. As Air Vice Marshal Lloyd, commander of RAF Malta put it, 'Every aeroplane in Sicily seemed to be flying round the island!'

Breconshire survived at least 11 separate attacks, but at 0920hrs, when halfway through the swept channel, a near miss exploded on hitting the water off the ship's starboard quarter. This caused flooding in the engine room, putting it temporarily out of action. The crew of *Carlisle* began preparing to take *Breconshire* under tow, while still trying to fend off further air attacks. By this stage, *Carlisle* was almost out of ammunition, and the three Hunts were running low. The rough seas made it impossible to pass a towline. At 0950hrs, *Penelope* appeared. The cruiser's commander, Capt. Nicholl, recalled, 'The *Breconshire* was hit. Her engines were put out of action, and she lost all electrical power ... The *Penelope* then managed to pass a towing wire, but in the full gale this soon parted.' A combination of the gale-force seas and the hefty displacement of *Breconshire* had proved too much.

Breconshire was saved from disaster by the quick thinking of Capt. Hutchinson. Before the towline parted, he had already prepared an anchor, just in case. He was now less than a mile and a half from the south-east corner of the island, having passed through the swept channel. So, he dropped anchor, to avoid being driven onto the lee shore by the gale. Hutchinson anchored the disabled *Breconshire* just off Il-Bajja ta' Marsaxlokk (Marsaxlokk Bay) near the Fleet Air Arm base at Kalafrana. There it weathered the storm, guarded by the three Hunts anchored around it. *Penelope* and *Carlisle* continued into Valletta, as did *Kingston* and *Havock*.

The lumbering *Clan Campbell* was less fortunate. *Clan Campbell* and the Hunt-class escort destroyer HMS *Eridge* were still 50 miles to the south-east of Malta when they first came under attack. It was 0720hrs. These were all fought off, but at 1020hrs, the freighter's luck ran out. It suffered a direct hit from a bomb dropped by a Ju 88, and the ship's back was broken. *Clan Campbell* began sinking, as the rough seas helped work open its wound. The freighter sank about 20 minutes later. However, Lt Cdr William Gregory-Smith of *Eridge* circled the area, regardless of the gale-force winds and two air attacks, and successfully rescued 112 survivors – the majority of the freighter's crew and passengers. When *Legion* went to help, the destroyer was attacked and then badly damaged by a near miss. Cdr Jessel limped into Marsaxlokk Bay and beached *Legion* close to the anchored *Breconshire*.

That marked the end of the operation, and the final homecoming of the convoy. Of its four ships, one, *Clan Campbell* had been sunk, but the three others had reached Malta, albeit two of them were damaged, and one of them was forced to anchor a few miles short of its destination. As night fell on D+3, and as Vian's Force B approached Alexandria, the whole operation was regarded as a success. During the engagement, which became known as the Second Battle of Sirte, R. Adm. Vian's cruisers and destroyers had held off a much more powerful foe, which included a battleship, and had successfully protected the convoy. It was little wonder that in Alexandria, Adm. Cunningham was pleased with the outcome of the whole operation. The trouble was, despite Second Sirte being a clear British defensive victory, any strategic benefit from it was swept away over the days that followed amid a welter of Axis bombs.

AFTERMATH

At 1215hrs on 24 March, the bulk of R. Adm. Vian's Force B (*Cleopatra*, *Euryalus* and *Dido*, plus *Hasty*, *Hero*, *Jervis*, *Kelvin*, *Kipling*, *Sikh* and *Zulu*) entered Alexandria, where its ships were cheered as they passed the two damaged battleships and dropped anchor. Cdr Wilfrid Woods on Adm. Cunningham's staff remembered the admiral's response to the cheering, 'ABC was unnaturally silent at first, but then all his delight burst out, and he cheered with the rest of us.' Later, Cunningham wrote, 'They had a wonderful reception, being enthusiastically cheered by the crews of all of the warships and merchant vessels in the harbour.' He added, 'I shall always consider the Battle of Sirte on March 22nd 1942 as one of the most brilliant naval actions of the war, if not the most brilliant.' This was a view shared by the British press and public alike, and by Prime Minister Churchill, who personally thanked Cunningham and the whole Mediterranean Fleet for their endeavours. This jubilation, though, proved a little premature.

After the battle, and the return of Vian's force to Alexandria, Adm. Cunningham paid a surprise visit to HMS *Jervis*, flotilla leader of the 14th Destroyer Flotilla. Here, the admiral is greeted by Capt. Albert Poland, who had been taken by surprise and was enjoying a well-deserved bath when the admiral arrived. He was forced to greet Cunningham in his dressing gown, but quickly changed into full uniform for this photograph.

The crew of HMS *Euryalus* lined the ship's sides during Force B's return to Alexandria on 24 March. Here, on the small quarterdeck, a Royal Marine band prepare to play, watched by a division of sailors and petty officers. Further astern down the buoyed channel is HMS *Dido*, the third ship in the cruiser squadron to enter port.

The air attacks on and around Malta on 23 March were part of a new bombing offensive by Fliegerkorps II, begun on 20 March, which targeted the island's airfields, harbours and coastal defences. The Luftwaffe averaged 300 bomber sorties a day over the island. These continued on 24 and 25 March, but this time the three merchant ships from the convoy were added to the list of targets. On Wednesday 25 March, *Breconshire* was towed to Marsaxlokk, where unloading begun. *Legion* was towed into Valletta. Air cover was provided, and for a time, the frequent air attacks were thwarted. However, the following day, 26 March, *Pampas* was bombed and sunk as the freighter lay in the southern end of Valletta's Grand Harbour. *Talabot* was set ablaze, and as the ship was carrying munitions, it was decided to scuttle the freighter to prevent a greater disaster. *Legion* was also hit by two bombs while lying alongside a wharf, and the ship's after magazine detonated. The destroyer capsized and sank, with its bridge resting on the quayside.

On 27 March, *Breconshire* was finally hit after four days of bombing. The ship sank in shallow water off Marsaxlokk. Most of *Breconshire*'s cargo of fuel was saved, but the work of unloading the two freighters had only just begun when they were sunk. Local dockworkers had refused to unload them during air attacks, and the soldiers drafted in to replace them made slow work of the task. In all, only 5,000 tons of stores were recovered before the ships sank – a quarter of their cargo. However, another 3,000–4,000 tons were recovered from the wrecks. Afterwards, Vian's flag

HMS *Breconshire*, pictured in Malta's Valletta harbour. Despite being damaged during its final approach to Malta, much of the fast supply ship's cargo of fuel oil was transferred ashore before the battered ship was sunk in an air attack on 27 March. More was salvaged afterwards.

captain argued that if the three ships had been deliberately beached, then almost all of the 26,000 tons of their cargo could have been saved. Capt. Hutchinson of *Breconshire* also suggested that his fast 18kt ship should have made the run on its own, without being tied to the lumbering *Clan Campbell*. Still, the cargo that did survive was enough to keep Malta in the fight for another three months. The island's ordeal wasn't over, but at least it had been thrown a temporary lifeline.

To avoid the air attacks on Valletta, *Carlisle* and four ships of the 5th Destroyer Flotilla (*Beaufort*, *Dulverton*, *Eridge* and *Hurworth*) sailed for Alexandria on 25 March and arrived there safely four days later. Back in Malta, *Penelope* was damaged in an air attack on the following day, 26 March, and remained in Valletta's dry dock, but was damaged again in further raids. On 29 March, *Avon Vale* left for Gibraltar, escorting the damaged cruiser *Aurora*, a Force K cruiser that had been under repair in Valletta. On 5 April, *Havock* made its escape from Malta, but ran aground on the Tunisian coast the following morning and was wrecked. Three days later, on 8 April, *Penelope* was patched up sufficiently to sail under cover of darkness, and despite further air attacks, the battered cruiser reached Gibraltar two days later. *Penelope*'s hull, riddled with holes from bomb splinters, earned the cruiser the nickname 'HMS *Pepperpot*'. The last victim from Vian's force was the destroyer *Kingston*, which was hit by a bomb from a Ju 87 Stuka and sank alongside the dock.

Despite these British losses at the hands of the Luftwaffe, the Italian battlefleet didn't return home unscathed. After the battle, it was caught by the full blast of the storm as it headed back to Taranto. On Monday 23 March (D+3), as the British convoy was fighting its way into Malta, the mountainous seas claimed two destroyers and their crews, *Lanciere* and *Scirocco*. *Lanciere* began foundering at 0958hrs and sank 18 minutes later.

The destroyer HMS *Kipling*, pictured on its return to Alexandria on 24 March after weathering the gale that followed the battle. The whole of Vian's Force B were cheered home by the sailors of the Mediterranean Fleet, in celebration of their achievement in driving off the Italian battlefleet and protecting the convoy.

Only 30 of its 206-strong crew were rescued. *Scirocco* shared the same fate. The destroyers *Geniere* and *Scirocco* had been sent out from Taranto to escort *Littorio* home. Only two of the *Scirocco*'s crew survived their ship's foundering. *Bande Nere* could have gone the same way, having been badly battered by the storm, but it managed to stay afloat, and eventually limped into Messina on 24 March. The cruiser was sunk off Stromboli the following month by a British submarine, while heading to La Spezia for repairs. Even *Littorio* made heavy weather of it during its return to Taranto, and suffered damage to its railings and superstructure. The storm had inflicted more damage to Iachino's battlefleet than the battle itself.

As for Malta, the siege continued, and on 15 April, King George VI awarded the people of Malta the George Cross for their heroism. However, this didn't help to feed them or fend off the bombers. The air attacks continued, but the arrival of Spitfires in April and May helped RAF Malta to fight back. Axis plans to invade the island were shelved, ironically thanks to the success of Rommel in the Western Desert. His attack in late May led to the capture of Tobruk and saw the British driven back through Egypt to El Alamein, just 50 miles from Alexandria. The support of Rommel became a greater priority than the capture of Malta, which gave the Allies some breathing space. In August, the Pedestal Convoy fought its way through to Valletta, as did further supply runs, and once again the island was used as a base from which to interdict Axis convoys. This led directly to the shortage of Rommel's supplies at El Alamein, which in turn contributed to his defeat there in November. Malta had managed to hold out, and this was due in part to the efforts of Convoy MW-10, and Vian's exemplary defence of it in the naval battle fought in a rising gale off the Gulf of Sirte.

THE BATTLEFIELD TODAY

Naturally, nothing remains of the battle, save for the scattered detritus of war on the seabed. However, the National War Museum in Valletta, housed in Fort St Elmo holds artefacts relating to the battle, including those from HMS *Breconshire*, HMS *Legion* and other participants in the Second Battle of Sirte. In Britain, the National Museum of the Royal Navy in Portsmouth Dockyard, the National Maritime Museum in Greenwich and the Imperial War Museum in London all have objects, displays, archival records and recordings that help tell the story of this unusual naval battle. In Italy, the Naval Technical Museum at La Spezia and the Naval History Museum in Venice both contain ship models, paintings and artefacts relating to the Regia Marina during this period, and tell the story of the building and careers of the battlefleet's battleships, cruisers and destroyers. As for aircraft, two complete Junkers Ju 88s survive in the RAF Museum in Hendon in London and the National Museum of the United States Air Force in Dayton, Ohio. The RAF Museum also has a complete Ju 87 Stuka in its collection. As for Italian aircraft, several examples, including an Ro.43 floatplane of the kind that first sighted the British convoy, can be found at the Italian Air Force Museum at Vigna di Valle to the north-west of Rome. Then, still on the seabed, their sites located and protected, are the remains of some of the ships involved in this story: *Clan Campbell*, *Bande Nere*, *Heythrop*, *Lanciere* and *Scirocco*. All also serve as the last resting place of many of their crew.

FURTHER READING

Bragadin, Marc'Antonio, *The Italian Navy in World War II*, Annapolis MD: United States Naval Institute (1957)
Brescia, Maurizio, *Mussolini's Navy: A Reference Guide to the Regia Marina 1930–45*, Barnsley: Seaforth Publishing (2012)
Campbell, John, *Naval Weapons of World War Two*, London: Conway Maritime Press (1985)
Freidman, Norman, *Naval Radar*, London: HarperCollins (1981)
Friedman, Norman, *British Cruisers: Two World Wars and After*, Barnsley: Seaforth Publishing (2010)
Friedman, Norman, *Naval Firepower: Battleship Guns and Gunnery in the Dreadnought Era*, Barnsley: Seaforth Publishing (2013)
Gardiner, Robert (ed.), *Conway's All the World's Fighting Ships, 1922–1946*, London: Conway Maritime Press (1980)
Gardiner, Robert (ed.), *The Eclipse of the Big Gun: The Warship, 1906–45*, Conway's History of the Ship Series, London: Conway Maritime Press (1992)
Greene, Jack & Massignani, Alessandro, *The Naval War in the Mediterranean 1940–43*, Rochester: Chatham Publishing (1998)
Grove, Eric, *Sea Battles in Close-Up*, 2 Vols, Shepperton: Ian Allen Ltd (1988, 1993)
Heathcote, Tony, *The British Admirals of the Fleet 1734–1995*, Barnsley: Pen & Sword (2002)
Lavery, Brian, *Churchill's Navy: The Ships, Men and Organisation 1939–45*, London: Conway (2006)
Ministry of Information, *The Mediterranean Fleet: Greece to Tripoli – The Admiralty Account of Naval Operations, April 1941 to January 1943*, London: HMSO (1944)
Morris, Douglas, *Cruisers of the Royal and Commonwealth Navies*, Liskeard: Maritime Books (1987)
O'Hara, Vincent, *Struggle for the Middle Sea: The Great Navies at War in the Mediterranean 1940–45*, London: Conway Maritime Press (2009)
Pack, S.W., *The Battle of Sirte*, Shepperton: Ian Allen Ltd (1975)
Preston, Anthony (ed.), *Jane's Fighting Ships of World War II*, London: Bracken Books (1989; originally published London: Jane's Publishing Company 1947)
Roberts, John, *British Warships of the Second World War*, Barnsley: Seaforth Publishing (2017)
Roskill, Stephen W., *The War at Sea*, Vols. 1, 2 & 3, History of the Second World War Series, London: HMSO (1954)
Sadkovitch, James, *The Italian Navy in World War II*, Santa Barbara, CA: Praeger Publishing (1994)
Whitley, M.J., *Cruisers of World War Two: An International Encyclopaedia*, London: Arms & Armour Press (1985)

INDEX

Figures in **bold** refer to illustrations.

air attacks 5, 10, 11, 13, **24**, 25, 26–27, 37, 39, 41, 53, 58–59, 66, 67, 87–88
aircraft 29
    floatplanes 21, 25, 30, 42, 94
    Ju 88 42, **43**, 53, **54**, 58, 66, 67, **83**, 87, 94
    SM.79 Sparviero **24**, 67, **67**
Avon Vale, HMS 32, **32**, 33, 41, 43, 45, 53, 53–54, 55, 58, 59, 67, 91

Barham, HMS 11, 20, **29**
battle details and description
    aftermath 89–92
    battlefield today 94
    Cleopatra shelled 59, **60–61**, 62, 63
    D-Day and D+1 34–41, **40**
    final events 84–88
    first contact with the enemy 22 March 1942 43–54, **44**, **48–49**, 50
    main encounter 22 March 1942 **56–57**
    'Medina Melee' 71–84, **72–73**
    Operation *MG-1* 32–33
    second contact 55–71
    torpedo attack on *Littorio* **76–77**, 78, 81, 82–84
battle plans
    Regia Marina 29–30
    Royal Navy 26–29
Beaufort, HMS 32, 33, 55, 91
'Bomb Alley' 13, **22**, 26–27, 30, 35, 36
bombing raids 4, **4**, **6**, 28, 30, 35, 42
    on Malta 87–88, 90
bombs **43**
Bragadin, Marco 12
Breconshire, HMS 12, 13, 34, 42, 86, 87–88, **87**, 90–91, **91**, 94
Bush, Capt. Eric 21, **22**, 42, 43, 46, 66

campaign chronology 7–8
campaign origins 9–13, **14**
Carlisle, HMS 34, **41**, 43, 45, 53, 53–54, 55, 58, 59, 67, 86, 87, 88, 91
casualties and losses 10, 65, 79–80, 88, 90–92
Churchill, Winston 70, 89
Clan Campbell, SS 13, 34–35, 36, 86, 87, 88, 94
Cleopatra, HMS 11, 13, **13**, 17, 20, 37, **37**, 38, 45, 46–47, **48–49**, 50, 51, 52, 53, **53**, 54, **54**, 59, 63–64, 66, 69–70, 75, 85
    hit by 6in shell 59, **60–61**, 62, 63
commanders
    Regia Marina 17–19
    Royal Navy 15–17
Conte di Cavour 5, 36
convoys 5–6, 11, 12, 13, 20, 26–27, 30, **79**, 93
    MW-10 17, 20, **22**, **31**, 32–39, 41–46, 44, 52–53, 55, 58–59, 63, 64–65, 67, 71, 84, 85–88, **86**
Cunningham, Adm. Sir Andrew B. 10, 11, 13, 15–16, **15**, 17, 20, 26, 27, 41, 86, 88, 89, **89**

Davidson, Gnr Bill 79, 80
destroyers, weapons layout **35**
Dido, HMS 20, 21, 45, 46, **46**, 47, 52, 53, 54, 59, 63–64, 66, 69, 70, **90**
    weapons layout **64**
Dulverton, HMS 32, 33, 55, 91

Ellis, Able Seaman John 80, 82
engines **68**
Eridge, HMS 32, 33, 55, 88, 91
Euryalus, HMS **11**, 20, 21, **22**, 37, 42, 43, 45, 46–47, **48–49**, 50, 51, 52, 53, 54, **54**, **58**, 59, **60–61**, 62, 63–64, 64, 65, 66, 69, 70, 75, **90**
Fleet Air Arm 10, 28, 36
Force B 34, 36
Force H 9–10, 29, 36
Force K 11, 27, 38, 42, 46
Fraatz, Olt Georg-Werner 33

Giovanni delle Bande Nere 20, 21, **21**, 23, 24, 45, **48–49**, 50, 51, 52, 59, **60–61**, 62, **63**, 69, 92, 94
Giulio Cesare 5, 18
Gorizia 20, 23, 45, **45**, 46, **48–49**, 50, 51, **51**, 52, 55, 69, 79
Grantham, Capt. Guy 21, 37, 46, 70
Gray, Plt Off Colin 85
Gulf of Sirte 4, 27, 30
guns 20–21, 22–24, **22**, **35**, **48–49**, 50, 51–52, **51**, 65, 66, 68, 74, **85**
    ammunition 58, 67
    fire control radars 20, **39**, 58, 64, **64**, **66**, 70
    range 47
    shelling of *Cleopatra* 59, **60–61**, 62, 63
    weapons layout on Dido-class cruisers **64**

Hasty, HMS 34, 45, 46, 51, **52**, 66–67, 69
Havock, HMS 34, 45, 51, 65, 68, 86, 88, 91
Hero, HMS 34, 45, 51, 65, 68, 75, **75**, 84
Heythrop, HMS 32, 33, 94
Hurworth, HMS 32, 33, 91
Hutchinson, Capt. Colin 34, 36, 42–43, 86, 88, 91

Iachino, Adm. Angelo 9, 10, 12, 17–19, **17**, 22, 23, 24, 30, 37, 43, 45, 46, 55, **55**, 59, 63, 64–65, 66, 67–68, 69, 83, 84–85

intelligence 29, 51

Jellicoe, Cdr Christopher 32, 33, 35, 43, 67
Jervis, HMS **27**, 35–36, 45, 69, 71, 74, **76–77**, 78, 80, 82, **89**
Jessel, Cdr Richard 38, 43, 88

Kelvin, HMS 45, 71, **74**, **76–77**, 78, **79**, 82
Kimberley, HMS **70**
Kingston, HMS 45, **76–77**, 78, 79–80, 82, **82**, 83, 86, 88, 91
Kipling, HMS 45, 71, **76–77**, 78, **92**

Lanciere 24, 91–92, 94
Legion, HMS 11, 27, 38, 42, 43, 46, 52, 71, **76–77**, 78, 82, 86, 88, 90, 94
Littorio 9, 12, **12**, 17, 22, 23, 24, 30, 43, 46, 55, 59, 63, 64, 65, 66, 68, 69–71, 74, 75, 79, **79**, 83
    torpedo attack on **76–77**, 78, 81, 82–84
Lively, HMS 34, 45, 51, 65, 68, 75, 83, 84
Long Range Desert Group 28, 35
Luftwaffe 10, 13, 25, 30, 34, 42, 90

McCall, Capt. Henry 21, 46
Malta 4, 9–10, 12–13, 26, 30, 87–88, 90–91, 93
Micklethwait, Capt. St John 34, **34**, 45, 59, 63, 64, 65–66, 67–68, 71, 83–84
mines 11
Moss, Lt John 75, 82
Mussolini, Benito 9, **9**, 10, 18

Naiad, HMS 13, 17, 21, 37
Naples 18
Neame, Capt. Douglas 34
Nicholl, Capt. Angus 27, 38, 39, 46, 52, 88
night fighting 12, 24, 84
North Africa 10, 12, 26

opposing forces 20–25
    Regia Marina 22–25
    Royal Navy 20–22
orders of battle 25

Pampas, MV 34, 86, **86**, 87, 90
Parona, V. Adm. Angelo 19, **19**, 23, 30, 43, 45, 46, 47, **48–49**, 50, 51, 52–53, 54, 55, 66
Penelope, HMS 21, 27, 38, 46, 52, 54, 59, 63–64, 66, **66**, 69, 70, 86, **87**, 88, 91
Poland, Capt. Albert 45–46, 51, 59, 67, 69, 71, 74, 75, 82, **89**

Queen Elizabeth, HMS 11, 20

radar 12, 24, **35**, **38**
    fire control radars 20, **39**, 58, 64, **64**, **66**, 70
reconnaissance 21, 24, 29–30, 35, 36
Regia Aeronautica 24, 30, 34, 39, 41
Regia Marina 5–6, **5**, 9–10, 12, 16, 17–19, 20, 37, 43, **44**, 45, 91–92, 94
    battle plans 29–30
    commanders 17–19
    doctrine 24
    first contact with Royal Navy 43–54, **44**, **48–49**, 50
    forces 22–25
    main encounter 22 March 1942 **56–57**
    'Medina Melee' **72–73**, 74
    orders of battle 25
Rommel, Erwin 10, 12, 26, 93
Royal Air Force (RAF) 13, 27, 28, 29, 34, 35, 38–39
Royal Navy 15–17, 20–22, **44**
    5th Destroyer Flotilla 32–33, 35, 91
    22nd Destroyer Flotilla 34, 52
    battle plans 26–29
    commanders 15–17
    first contact with the enemy 22 March 1942 43–54, **44**, **48–49**, 50
    forces 20–22
    main encounter 22 March 1942 **56–57**
    'Medina Melee' 72–73, 74
    Mediterranean Fleet 5, 9–10, 15–16, 20
    orders of battle 25

Scirocco 91–92, 93, 94
Sikh, HMS 21, 34, 45, 51, 52, 59, 64, 65, 68, 75, 84
Sirte, First Battle of 5, 12, 18, 30
Sirte, Second Battle of 5–6, 18–19, 88
    see also campaign details
smokescreens 41, 43, 46, **47**, **48–49**, 50, 51, **52**, 53, 59, **60–61**, 62, 63–64, 65, 67–68, 70, 71, 83
Somerville, Lt Cdr Philip 80, **82**
Southwold, HMS 32, 33, 55
submarines 11, 19, 26, 29, **33**, 33
Supermarina 10, 18, 29–30

Talabot, M/S 34, 86, 87, 90
'Tobruk Run' 28
torpedoes 21, 24, **29**, 33, **35**, 65, **67**, 68, 69, 70, 71, 75
    anti-torpedo systems 23, 83
    attack on *Littorio* **76–77**, 78, **81**, 82–84
    torpedo teams 80
Trento 20, 23, **23**, 24, 45, **48–49**, 50, 51, 69, 74
Tribal-class destroyers **69**, 85

U-boats *see* submarines

Valletta **4**, 5, 6
Valiant, HMS 11, **20**
Vian, R. Adm. Sir Philip 5–6, 12, 13, 16–17, **16**, 19, 21–22, 27, **27**–28, 30, 36, 37–38, 41–42, 43, **48–49**, 50, 51, 55, 58–59, 63–64, 66–67, 69, 70–71, 85
    'Enemy Driven Off' signal 54
    flagship shelled 59, **60–61**, 62, 63
    pre-arranged plan 45–46

Zulu, HMS 21, 34, 45, 46, 51, 52, **52**, 66–67, 69